ESCAPE FROM SMOKING

LOOK YOUNGER
FEEL YOUNGER
MAKE MONEY
& LOVE YOUR LIFE!

TIM WILLIAMSON

Wrightbooks

First published 2010 by Wrightbooks, an imprint of
John Wiley & Sons Australia, Ltd
42 McDougall Street, Milton Qld 4064

Office also in Melbourne

Typeset in Berkeley LT 12/15.4pt

National Library of Australia Cataloguing-in-Publication data:

Author:	Williamson, Tim (Timothy Andrew), 1974-
Title:	Escape from smoking: look younger, feel younger, make money and love your life! / Tim Williamson.
ISBN:	9781742169934 (pbk.)
Notes:	Includes index.
Subjects:	Smoking cessation. Smoking cessation—Health aspects. Self-care, Health.
Dewey number:	616.86506

Cover design by Xou Creative.

Cover image © iStockphoto.com/darklord_71

Printed in Australia by McPherson's Printing Group

10 9 8 7 6 5 4 3 2 1

John Wiley & Sons Australia, Ltd places great value on the environment and is actively involved in efforts to preserve it. The paper used in the production of this book was supplied by mills that source their raw materials from sustainably managed forests.

Disclaimer

The material in this publication is of the nature of general comment only, and does not represent professional advice. It is not intended to provide specific guidance for particular circumstances and it should not be relied on as the basis for any decision to take action or not take action on any matter which it covers. Readers should obtain professional advice where appropriate, before making any such decision. To the maximum extent permitted by law, the author and publisher disclaim all responsibility and liability to any person, arising directly or indirectly from any person taking or not taking action based upon the information in this publication.

Contents

About the author

Tim has flown as a commercial pilot in three countries. He's an experienced business owner, fitness coach, martial arts instructor and masseur with a passion for health, fitness and teaching.

A car accident in 2002 saw him grounded from flying and unable to continue fitness coaching so he has since studied many different areas of business and personal development.

Acknowledgements

I would like to acknowledge the following people:

My Dad—thanks for believing in me and in yourself.

My Mum—thanks for your fantastic support.

Nick—thanks for your insights into fires that have helped me write this book.

Joe—thanks for your insights into the human body and eating properly.

Sandy—thanks for your guidance and help over the years.

Nicole—many thanks for your wonderful support—even during the midnight torch-lit note-writing sessions under the quilt.

Introduction
Let's get started

Congratulations on making the choice to start this program. You're about to help yourself look younger, feel younger, gain financial success and improve your life exponentially. More importantly, you're going to be able to help others and the world around you.

I'll take you on a journey through the human psyche and physical body for you to learn the effects and implications of smoking. You will understand and defeat smoking—you have been a slave to it for too long. By the end of this book you will have the knowledge, reasoning, beliefs, strategies and tools to help you stop smoking.

We will follow a structured format which will allow you to absorb and utilise the information in the most effective way. I'll take you through some familiar territory and explore some options you may not have considered. This is an interactive program so there's space for you to pen your responses to any questions I pose throughout this book. After you have completed the program once from cover to cover you may re-visit any section you wish to clarify or reinforce any points.

How it will work for you will depend upon how you apply yourself to the next few hours — you'll need to give it your all to see the benefits.

You need to enter this program with:

- a relaxed, refreshed mind

- a view to gaining a new lease of life and enjoying yourself more

- the prospect of gaining more time and energy to achieve the things you want and desire

- no preconceived ideas about stopping smoking

- a willingness to participate fully and follow all of the instructions given.

After I finished writing *Escape from Debt* my father came to me with some research material and one request: to write a book that would help him to stop smoking. It is his belief in my ability to teach (I have taught martial arts and fitness successfully since the age of 16) that has helped me to complete this program. The fact that I care about him and have seen the troubles he has gone through in his particular journey has made this book a true labour of love. Not only the trust and belief in yourself but also your trust in me and belief in my abilities will allow you to successfully enter this new phase of your life.

I'm going to show you how to free your mind from a program that has had you in its clutches for too long. I will teach you to be able to shift your focus and energy to more worthwhile pursuits—your family, friends, self-improvement, health and weight loss to name a few. I'll show you how the brain works and how the links to substances that make you 'feel good' are created. By understanding how links are created and how they work you can consciously be aware of their power to switch you into automatic mode. This new level of awareness will give you the strength to make the changes you require.

You will be able to begin and complete the transition without spending another cent of your hard-earned money. I'm going to show you how you can get the most out of your life and have as much as you desire.

It is my belief you will find the trigger today that will detonate the old program and create a new and empowered life.

This will be a completely natural solution with the only side effects listed as:

- a sense of inner strength

- a heightened feeling of self-belief

- a feeling of complete resolution

- more time for you to enjoy your life and the people around you.

Today it will be you who wins.

Instructions

It's time now to get prepared. Here is what you will need:

1   A pen, preferably red, green or blue so that it contrasts against the black ink on these pages.

2   A box of white tissues (you'll see why later, and no, I'm not going to upset you!).

3   Your cigarettes and your lighter/matches.

4   A waste basket.

5   A tennis ball or soft rubber ball.

6   A glass of cold, filtered or spring water (no ice — squeeze of lemon juice is optional). Coffee, tea, juice, alcohol and carbonated or sugary drinks are not going to help you to concentrate as they all contain stimulants.

7   A 'Do Not Disturb' sign. You do not wish to be disturbed for a few hours.

8   A few hours. Did the previous point give this one away? I know you are busy so I have designed this program to be as quick (yet effective) as possible.

There are just a few things I will ask you to do as you work with me on this program.

Empty your mind of any preconceived ideas

Watching a child learn a new skill is incredible. They have no preconceived ideas or failures to draw upon so they proceed without doubt or prejudice. It's time for you to remember when you had no fear or doubts. Use the power of that memory to focus on all that you can gain in the near future.

Reflect regularly

I really encourage you to not just read but to stop regularly and reflect upon what you have experienced. By drawing comparisons or by telling your own story in your mind (or to someone you care about, and who cares about you) it is my belief that you will be able to escape from smoking with very little physical and mental effort.

Be actively involved

A number of questions and exercises have been included in this book. By following the instructions the connection you will make with the material will be far greater than if you were to just read through the text and skim over the top. This book will have its desired effect if you immerse yourself completely rather than just sit on top like a mosquito does on a pond of water.

Have a clear objective

When you are clear about where you want to go or what you want to achieve it will be easier to make it happen.

What do you really want to achieve by reading this book? Write your answer here.

....

....

Don't be distracted

You'll need to sit in a quiet area with absolutely no distractions. Turn off your phone and anything in the background that may disturb you. Hang a 'Do Not Disturb' sign on your door. You're going to need to completely involve yourself for the next three to four hours.

Write your answers down

Write your answers in pen so that you cannot change them. This isn't an exam and there is no right or wrong answer to any question. Be honest and open with your answers.

Writing your answers and notes in this book will play an important part in:

- creating a personal history and remembering your journey

- removing ambiguity

- charting your progress and seeing the positive changes you have made

- providing an insight into how you are processing the information

- combining your senses and creating a bridge between your subconscious and conscious mind

- connecting the physical with the mental abilities

- improving your memory retention by up to 80 per cent.

Approach with an open mind

I am going to present to you some questions that will ask you to look deep inside yourself for an answer. You may not normally actively seek to confront yourself and your behaviour on purpose but I can tell you the rewards for doing so over the next few hours will be great.

What have you got to lose? Write your answer here.

....

....

Ask someone to work with you and be your support

When changing your patterns of behaviour and beliefs you will need to talk to someone who can help you through times of confusion. The human mind likes to feel safe and secure so when it goes through changes it sometimes will want to run back to the old behaviour. This confusion may result in a sense of irritability and frustration which may trigger a reversion to the old 'safe' program of smoking. It's times like these when you may want to chat with someone to clear your mind and regain your focus.

I know I can rely on and place my trust in ...

....

Take your time to fill out the questions below, review them and enjoy the thought of their attainment.

What do you believe you will gain from now on?

....

....

How do you believe your relationships with others will improve?

....

....

How will your work life improve?

....

....

How do you think your health will improve?

....

....

You have the potential right now to achieve anything you desire and you certainly have the potential to stop smoking today.

You must have the desire to want the change to happen for it to be effective. There is no treatment that will work if your desire to change is not present in the first place.

As a quick measure now I'd like to check your commitment to this program and the results you desire.

Remember that this is not a test and no-one else has to see what you have written. I need you to be honest so you can get a true measure in your mind.

On a scale of 1 to 10, how strongly do you feel that you honestly want to stop smoking right now? Circle your answer.

0   1   2   3   4   5   6   7   8   9   10

Low desire   Strong desire

For this program to be completely effective, where do you think your level of commitment and desire to stop smoking has to be?

0   1   2   3   4   5   6   7   8   9   10

Low desire   Strong desire

Here's some more questions I'd like you to answer as truthfully and honestly as possible. Are you ready?

Okay! Let's start by writing your answers to the questions below.

What would you like to achieve in your life?

....

....

Would you like to be successful with:

- your relationships with others?

- gaining success at work and a possible promotion?

- creating and following a personal weight loss program?

- increasing your general fitness?

- starting a successful new business or expanding your current business?

- connecting with your children and spending more time with them?

- finding a new level of self-awareness and confidence?

- buying your dream home?

- saving for the holiday of a lifetime?

What do you desire?

....

....

What makes you truly happy?

....

....

You can create your own success from the potential that is in you and surrounds you.

The time is now

Throughout my life I have found that time has different modes. There are periods where time seems to rocket past and you wonder where the hours have gone and then there are others when the ticking of the clock dominates your thoughts, second by second. I can tell you that no time moves more slowly for me than when I am hungry and waiting for a meal to cook. You've no doubt heard the old adage 'a watched kettle never boils'. Time is how we perceive it. Time isn't a thing or something that happens. It is simply a means of how we each measure segments of our lives.

Time is an interesting concept and many teachers say to live for now because the future doesn't exist and the past is gone. History is important because we can look back and glean the lessons from many situations. These lessons can influence our thinking or actions and point us in the right direction for the future. Something I believe a lot of people find hard to define is what *now* means.

By the time you have read this your *now* may be in the past or it may still be happening, so is now 'now' or is now ... 'now'?

Confused yet? I'm not trying to complicate things but just show you that *your time is how you consciously perceive it and how you make the best use of it.*

How many times have you been so immersed in a task that you have looked up at the clock and wondered where the last few hours went? Life is a ceaseless dance and exchange of energy so how do we embrace or take control of it? How can we make it work for us instead of just getting caught up in the flow? How can we make the most of our lives and avoid the feeling of being stuck or stagnant?

The first step in taking control is awareness. It's time to open your eyes to new possibilities and consciously make decisions to move ahead and step up in the levels that life has for us. To make the most of your life and to create the changes that you desire you need to know that you can make those changes and you can start the process this very minute.

Recently I was woken in the middle of the night with a vexing question. People say we should 'live for now', but what is now and what does it mean to you?

Is now the split second it takes to realise the instant you are in?

Is now five minutes?

Is now 10 hours?

Is now six months?

Is now 80 years?

Is now just the time it takes for our conscious mind to break free from the subconscious routines of day-to-day life to look around and smell the roses?

My point here is to open your conscious mind to the concept of 'now', take a strong hold of your life and make the decision to be in control and enjoy every aspect. You can even enjoy the truly challenging times by enjoying and valuing the lessons they have to teach.

Is now your time?

Is the time right to escape from smoking?

Absolutely!

Consciously take hold of 'now' with both hands and hold on tight. Here we go.

An easy scientific experiment for you

I know that you have a packet of cigarettes there. What you will need for this activity is a cigarette and a tissue.

This will take approximately two minutes.

Place the tissue over the filter end of the cigarette and put it up to your lips. Try to keep your lips and the tissue dry during this experiment.

Light the cigarette and smoke it as normal through the tissue.

With each puff you take move the end of the cigarette to a new part of the tissue. This will be easy to see when you do it.

Be sure to smoke the entire cigarette through the tissue so you get a complete picture.

Remove the cigarette and tissue. Extinguish the butt and examine the tissue.

What do you observe on the tissue?

What do you observe at the end of the cigarette filter?

Was the filter effective?

You will notice that it has filtered only a portion of the gunk that you would normally inhale.

Now be aware that this is only one cigarette. How many do you smoke each day?

Just a little bit of maths for you. Multiply the gunk on the tissue by how many cigarettes you have each day.

Now multiply that by 365.

Has this given you reason why you should be working your hardest to stop smoking?

If you believed that the filters caught most of the 'tar' then this will show you some of what's really happening.

Chapter 1

THE ACCIDENT CHAIN AND PROGRAMS OF BEHAVIOUR

You alone must do it, but you can't do it alone.

O Hobart Mowrer

Throughout my flying career I have been educated in many areas of human understanding in an effort to be able to make better decisions when in charge of many lives. The concept of the accident chain is something that has really had an impact on my life and I wish to share it with you now.

Imagine a chain, simple links that go together one by one to form a length. Chains can be made of different materials of variable thicknesses that affect the way they perform. This chain can be of any length. Disaster comes when the chain breaks. In an aircraft accident this can be catastrophic not just for the person, people or situation creating the links but also for the people around them.

The accident chain for an aircraft can begin forming with the decision to take off when the weather is not ideal. The links can accumulate if the pilot is tired or distracted by external factors. Perhaps a decision to not put enough fuel on board to get to safety if the destination runway is flooded or damaged will place another link in the chain. The pilot may become stressed by the thought of what may happen and may lose focus. This could be enough to misjudge the distance to a hillside, and then an accident happens. The chain breaks. Apply this accident chain theory to smoking and it begins at the first cigarette. Without knowing it you have just created a link. Then the second cigarette and the third have created new links. Chain-smoking establishes a weak link in your chain. You might then ignore concerns from your doctor or a family member and continue smoking when they have noticed irregularities in your behaviour or health.

For your chain to break and an accident to occur, the number and quality of links in your chain need to reach a point where the chain can no longer maintain its integrity.

Using this concept, can you see your accident chain being formed and where it may be strained? Write down some of your links below.

....

....

Can you identify any weak links?

....

....

The great thing about recognising the accident chain is that the formation of the chain can be stopped at any time, before it breaks. Recognition in itself can be curative.

Programs of behaviour

There are different arguments as to whether smoking is to be called an addiction or a habit, so from now on I am going to refer to it as a program of behaviour.

Our brains are incredible things we often unfortunately under uses and do not completely understand. They have evolved over tens of thousands of years to be learning and storage powerhouses. Like a robot that has been set to follow a continuous program, our brains run regular patterns so we can operate during our day and remain safely within our comfort zones.

In karate training we repeatedly practise the same physical actions and patterns of movement. As time passes, the physical actions become faster, more controlled and precise until they can be performed as a matter of programmed reflex. The brain has created a strong link to that movement and can trigger the body to perform it quickly and automatically.

Without going into a litany of scientific detail our brains work like a three-dimensional city with streets that interconnect in all directions. In our regular day there are paths that we travel often and there are others that we travel infrequently. Most of the brain remains untravelled but when we do take a new path we create a connection and a fresh neural pathway is born. If we travel that path only once, the link will be weak and may eventually fade until only a trace remains.

The strongest links are the ones we travel regularly and automatically without thinking. To be able to consciously perform every single daily action would overload our conscious minds so this automation has become a natural part of our makeup. The brain with all of these links cannot operate consciously all of the time as there are just far too many processes for us to be in control of every step of the way. This automation can show up in our everyday behaviour with unconscious patterns and actions such as nail biting, chewing the lower or upper lip, nose picking or constant 'sniffing', fidgeting or facial tics.

Have you ever driven your car down a regularly travelled road and suddenly become aware that you were lost in your thoughts and were operating in automatic mode? When you first drove a car you would have leap-frogged and ground the gears. Now you can drive, eat food and hold a conversation without giving much thought to your actions. Can you remember when you first smoked a cigarette? Do you remember what may have been your particular motivational factor for doing so? Was it to be like your favourite movie star? Was it to be rebellious? Were you simply curious? Was it to be like your friends and be accepted as a part of the group? Was it to be like your father? Did you want to feel like an adult, a feeling of 'growing up' and 'arriving'?

A lot of the smokers I have interviewed can recall when they began. A common link was the power of friends or role models and the peer pressure to feel as though they are a part of the group.

While sports is by far the best avenue to attract, sample and influence our core target smokers, it's not the only way. International movies and videos also have tremendous appeal to our young adult consumers in Asia.

Philip Morris internal document (1990) — sourced from WHO report on smoking 2008

The first cigarette you smoked created a new connection —a new neural pathway—and each cigarette that followed reinforced that link to create one that is now strong enough that you travel it automatically on a daily basis.

These regular highways can be diluted or weakened over time (which is the aim of patches, gum and other alternative methods), but some situations can arise to create immediate changes which can cause links to be instantly weakened and even severed.

Today is one of those opportunities to sever the link you have with smoking.

The links in our brain serve to satisfy our basic human need for comfort and continuity. As humans we love to be comfortable, and to put ourselves out of our zone can set the alarm bells ringing. It's time to silence the alarm bells (fear and doubt) and start to experience a few new things. I'm not going to ask you to lie on a bed of sharp nails, swim with sharks or wrestle live crocodiles but what I will do is ask you to look at some different ways of thinking and shift you out of your comfort zone. My objective is to get you to step off the regularly travelled highway and change your association with smoking.

It won't be too hard, will it?

By the end of this book you will be having fun with the techniques and will be hungry for opportunities to expand further.

When was the last time you were in a classroom or a gathering that went over a period of a few days? Did you notice that everyone prefers to sit in the same seat? Upon entering the room the scenery would have been unfamiliar. Therefore the first place you sat would have become a 'safety point' for you and the situation would have been the same for the other attendees. You would have become familiar with your particular view and this position is where you would have created your baseline, your reference to the new surroundings to which you would return every day thereafter.

I enjoy going into classrooms and training groups and moving around into different seats just to see what people's reactions are going to be. The most extreme reaction was that of a young man who threw me out of 'his' seat and hurled my bag across the room. Obviously it will take a bit more work for that particular individual to make any changes he requires in his life.

This illustrates what a habit, pattern of behaviour or a program can do to control our actions and kick in our defence mechanisms. Throughout our lives we perceive and interpret each experience to create certain conditions, rules and guidelines that we then follow until another experience comes along that causes us to change or amend our rules. In the case of the classroom the brain fixes a safety point and it is from this position that we refer to everything else.

The lessons are always presenting themselves to us but whether or not we are ready to see and accept them is the controlling factor as to whether we will change or not.

Dealing with the triggers

You may have been smoking for many years so it will be conditioned into your system as a regular program of behaviour. Light up, raise, puff, raise, puff, raise, puff, raise, puff, raise, puff, raise, puff, raise, puff, extinguish. Thirty times per day. Can you see how easily it can reinforce itself?

This program can and will have many factors that will set it off into automatic mode.

For example:

- when you wake up

- when you are bored

- before/after sex

- before a car or plane journey

- before or after a meal

- stressful situations.

There are going to be many things in the day that will trigger you to light up a cigarette and take that big, first drag.

Reflect now upon your regular day. What are the triggers and regular things that cause you to reach for a cigarette?

....

....

Resist the urge to reach for one now. I know that your subconscious trigger just kicked in.

Remember to breathe.

Why do you have a cigarette at those times?

....

....

How does that cigarette make you feel?

....

....

What are the physical sensations that you experience?

....

....

Being able to identify the triggers that cause you to smoke is a great way to be able to interrupt your smoking program. Linking your conscious mind with the subconscious, automatic triggers will enable you to realise when you are about to run your program and interrupt or cancel it before it takes control.

Could your unconscious triggers be a weak link in your accident chain?

Take some time now to sit and think about what causes you to light up. Be sure to write them down and add to the list as they come to you. Referring to this page will help you in the future.

What causes me to light up a cigarette?

....

....

If you are a *sometimes* or *social* smoker then you may realise that your pattern of behaviour is linked with social situations. You have a drink in one hand and a cigarette in the other but normally during the day you don't feel the *need* to light up.

Regular smokers will generally have set some subconscious rules for when they light up and may often light a cigarette without even realising it. I've witnessed smokers fumbling for their lighter and packet when they have already got a cigarette dangling from their lips. It's like fruitlessly searching all of the regular places you keep your sunglasses when they have been perched on your head the entire time.

Overly stressful situations will be a particular trigger for regular smokers. The word *stress* these days has become overused and associated with hard times and negative effects on the body and mind.

Stress can be defined as pressure, mental or physical strain, a system of forces producing or sustaining a strain, to exert pressure on, to emphasise.

It is here that I need to stress that 'stress' is perfectly normal and is necessary for us to grow both physically and mentally. In the building and repair of bones and muscle our bodies use stress in the form of torsion and strain. This strengthens and reinforces existing material as well as creates new structure and fibres. Mental stress helps us to exercise our brain and allows connections to be formed for the signals to pass through. Stress in normal amounts results in a calming effect and can even assist us in our sleep phase.

You can get too much of a good thing though. Too much mental and/or physical stress can have negative effects on the mind. Our bodies use stress to grow but when the stress becomes too much the effects can become destructive to our physical and mental wellbeing. One can experience symptoms such as:

- agitation

- depressive behaviour

- difficulty sleeping

- anxiety and worry

- reduced concentration and focus

- speaking or acting harshly towards those around you

- blood pressure problems

- external physical symptoms such as hair loss or discoloration.

We will each develop different methods for dealing with the normal levels of stress as well as the abnormal levels. It is how we deal with our stresses that will determine how our minds and bodies respond. Some people may interpret and express excess levels of stress more physically while others may simply repress any feelings or visible emotions. When overly stressed, we may feel as though our heads are being crushed in a vice while other times we may actually rise to the occasion and take the challenge head-on.

When smokers are stressed and reach for a cigarette, even the motion of doing so can have a calming effect before they even take that first drag. The act of inhaling deeply when taking that first drag allows oxygen to enter the body and the partnered effect of a nicotine-induced feeling of euphoria can allow smokers to calm their nerves rapidly. The basic human need for safety is found in the regular program of smoking, something that may have been a constant for smokers for years and been accepted as their 'de-stress program'.

Recognising how you deal with your daily stressors and the eventual excessively stressful moments can be instrumental in how you can change your pattern of behaviour to avoid reaching for a cigarette in the future.

Dealing with stress is important to being able to function properly in your daily life. There are tools and methods available for you to manage in your own way. You just need to discover what works for you.

Humans have a wonderful range of emotions and feelings and all of them have a purpose—to deny them can be damaging.

If you feel justifiably angry how do you express your anger?

....

....

If you feel sad, how do you express your feelings?

....

....

If you feel happy and elated, how do you express yourself?

....

....

Clear communication with others and understanding how you manage your feelings, emotions and everyday experiences can help you to live a balanced and healthy life.

Do you presently experience any of the symptoms such as anxiety, depressive behaviour, agitation, reduced concentration or difficulty sleeping?

....

....

Do you feel overly stressed at home or at work?

....

....

Do you feel tight in the chest or have difficulty breathing in stressful situations?

....

....

Do you experience headaches on a regular basis?

....

....

I will show you some coping methods but if you feel overly stressed at home or at work or are experiencing negative physical symptoms then it is important that you find a professional counsellor, psychologist or doctor. Openly communicating with someone you can trust and who can allow you to 'vent' in a controlled manner and help you find solutions is wonderfully curative. Instead of pills and potions I believe you should find someone who can guide you personally, teach you coping methods and show you how to solve the problems you face.

Chapter 2

WHAT IS NICOTINE?

Smoking is one of the leading causes of statistics.

Author unknown

In the following chapters we will discuss how smoking has affected the world around you, your life, your body and your mind. Before we begin, though, you should really understand one chemical: nicotine.

When diplomat Jean Nicot introduced tobacco to the French court in 1560, he would have had no idea that his name would be put to one of the most problematic substances in history.

The tobacco plant *Nicotiana tabacum* is related to the potato and tomato and is a member of the nightshade family. It can vary depending upon where it is grown with differences in climate, conditions and location resulting in a variety of colours, tastes, aromas, nicotine content and combustion properties.

Nicotine itself is a colourless and soluble liquid which is a naturally occurring insecticide that is deadly in its pure form. It can be manufactured synthetically and is naturally present in many plants although the tobacco variants hold the highest levels.

What does nicotine do?

When nicotine is released into the body, the brain becomes stimulated and this can provide sensations of relaxation, euphoria or a sensation of enhanced concentration. Physical symptoms in humans generally are constricted blood vessels, increased blood pressure, raised heart rate and changes in the signals within the central nervous system.

The levels of nicotine during smoking are at their highest within the first two minutes of each individual 'hit' but disappear very quickly. The act of repeatedly raising a cigarette to your lips over a period of a few minutes and taking multiple doses allows the nicotine level to compound and the poisonous drug to take a strong hold.

Because it is soluble, nicotine leaves your system relatively quickly, mostly within a matter of hours and almost completely within weeks. As the nicotine level dissipates the brain becomes hungry for the sensation the cigarette provides, the so-called craving kicks in for another cigarette and the program restarts. This hunger creates a series of ups and downs that are fed by the introduction of more nicotine or other stimulant like sugar or caffeine.

For years you have been running a subconscious roller-coaster program as well as strengthening and reinforcing it through the repetitive action of smoking a cigarette.

A lot of smokers feel they will be excused by explaining they are simply addicts and have no way of getting away from their habit. Addiction becomes a powerful excuse in their repertoire. You may have said it in jest but this may have been something your subconscious mind has filed for later use to protect itself from change.

The term 'addict' is defined as a person who is dependent upon a drug; 'addiction' means to devote or give oneself up to, to practise persistently. Now, it is my belief that in the case of smoking 'addiction' is a self-defeating term that reinforces the program your brain has accepted. To say you are 'addicted' is simply labelling the problem and allowing it to continue unhindered. If you want to have more power over what you do each day (I know you do because you would not otherwise be reading this book) then it is time to extinguish the term 'addict'. It is time to take control of yourself and of your actions.

It is easy to declare yourself an 'addict' and just give in to the excuse. I don't believe in labels or calling oneself an 'addict'. Don't be tempted to just accept your 'addiction'. Take it out of your repertoire and eliminate it as an excuse. Recognise that there is a reaction you have to a substance that your brain thinks it likes and you need to rediscover the natural sensations of pleasure, relaxation and relief from stress.

Now is the time to find something more empowering to replace the old program. You have got the strength and power within you to create the changes required.

Break time

It is now time for a quick break and a drink of *water*.

Coffee is an artificial stimulant and acts as a diuretic which means that you'll dehydrate easily. When paired up with the effects of smoking the two can create some real challenges for your body to work against.

Did you know that smokers tend to drink more coffee than non-smokers?

Does your body honestly *need* the caffeine?

If we did need nicotine or caffeine then wouldn't we have a gland or organ that naturally produced it when our body detected that we *needed* some?

Do you really *need* that cup of coffee in the morning to get you started, or have you just run the coffee program so many times that you don't even think about it any more?

At the start of this chapter, I mentioned that nicotine was soluble. This means that it will dissolve in water, so by increasing your water intake you can remove the nicotine from your system in a rapid, clean and natural fashion.

Increasing your water intake will increase the amount you urinate which is one method the body uses to remove toxins. An increase in the volume of water you ingest will not only assist your filtration and flushing system but also your bowels and other bodily functions.

Chapter 3

SMOKING AND THE BIGGER PICTURE

*Tobacco use is the leading preventable cause
of death in the world.*

World Health Organization: *The World Health Report 2003*

There are four different kinds of experiences in this world;
those that are:

1   good for us but bad for others

2   bad for us but good for others

3   good for us and good for others

4   bad for us as well as bad for others.

Over the course of our lives it's a pretty good bet that we
are going to do a combination of all of the above things.
Something that is bad for you as well as bad for others is,

let's say ... smoking. All right, we know that it's bad for us, the warnings tell us every time we look at the packets nowadays. Do you really need me to go on about that? No. I know you are intelligent enough to know what it does but just how big is the big picture?

The casualties of smoking

You may know that there are over 4000 chemical compounds in cigarette smoke. Two hundred of them are poisonous and 40 are known carcinogens. A poison can make you sick or even kill you in the right concentration and a carcinogen is known to cause cancer or is suspected of causing cancer in humans, depending on the rating of the carcinogen.

When it comes to cigarettes and smoking tobacco products it is not just about the nicotine in the tobacco. During manufacture there can potentially be hundreds of additives to the tobacco which can include flavourings and humectants (which keep the tobacco moist). Since cigarettes are not classified as a food or drug, the quantity and type of ingredients can remain undeclared. The manufacturing companies can safeguard their recipes and create whatever cocktails they wish. This is tragic in itself but the process of combustion changes all of these chemicals and bonding structures to create even more dangerous chemicals.

World Health Organization figures show that in the 20th century over 100 million people died due to smoking-induced illness. The projections for the 21st century are indicating over 1 billion deaths. What sort of impact does smoking have on the world's economies in terms of health care?

As the Asian and South American markets open up for the cigarette companies there are going to be big changes in these figures. A sick person in India, Indonesia or China costs very little to those countries' governments but will cost a lot in lost labour to family and friends who stop work to case for the person. The profit from the sales of cigarettes and the returns to the governments in taxes and excise will still increase because of the sheer population numbers but the spending on health care and public awareness campaigns will always be restricted by a budget. The implications are massive.

Governments around the world spend considerably less than they earn on health problems in terms of tax revenue. Some governments are proposing further increases to these taxes and I believe that to do so without justification or fair spending would further serve to penalise the people who choose to smoke. It has been recommended by health organisations around the world to increase taxes as a deterrent for smokers and for those considering starting. However, interviews with smokers have shown me that this will be counter-productive and only cause further economic strain on those who have made the choice.

I'm sure that if governments were to do a costing on the resources to perform regular clean-up operations for litter/proper disposal of smoking materials and for the continued health care required they could justify the action of raising taxes. Smokers may be initially reluctant to part with the extra cash but if they can see the justifiable results they can at least retain their dignity.

According to World Health Organization (WHO) figures in a report published by MPower in 2008, the number of annual tobacco-related deaths reached a total of almost 4 million people per year. The actual total is expected to be a lot higher considering that WHO does not cover every country in the world.

The Marlboro Men—casualties of marketing

In the 1950s and 1960s tobacco companies switched their target audience from females to males and the macho image of smoking emerged. The Baby Boomers grew up with the image of the tough cowboys riding across the range with a cigarette hanging from their mouths.

David McLean, who was one of the original Marlboro cowboys, began smoking at the age of 12. When he began his career as the Marlboro Man it was written into his contract that he was required to be seen smoking at all times. This clause in his contract meant that he smoked up to five packets per day. In 1985 he was diagnosed with emphysema and in 1993 doctors found he had lung cancer. In 1995 doctors discovered that the cancer had spread from his lungs to his spine and his brain. David died on 12 October 1995 in Los Angeles, California.

In 1996, David McLean's family took the giant tobacco company Philip Morris to court. This case was instrumental in opening the floodgates of litigation against the tobacco companies and making them somewhat accountable for their products, for example, printing warnings on cigarette packets and advertising.

Wayne McLaren, another famous Marlboro Man, was 51 when he died from lung cancer.

David Millar Jr, who was another Marlboro Man, died from emphysema in 1987.

Will Thornbury, the model for Camel, died from lung cancer in 1992 at the age of 57.

Janet Sackman was the Lucky Strike girl. She lost her voice box and part of her lung to cancer.

Does this dull the cool image?

You would think that the founders of a tobacco company would know better. RJ Reynolds Sr, who was the founder of the RJ Reynolds Tobacco Co., died at the age of 67 from pancreatic cancer in 1916. His son, RJ Reynolds Jr, was 58 when he died from emphysema, and RJ Reynolds III died from emphysema at the age of 60 in 1994.

Marketers love to target specific audiences with their advertising whether it is housewives, cowboy wannabes, children, sports fans or teenagers. A recent scandal in my home town came about when cigarette companies began to recruit hairdressers and beauty salons to become sellers of cigarettes and smoking products. The advertising of tobacco products is heavily regulated in Australia yet the marketers are always looking for an angle to latch on to a new audience. Needless to say the scheme was exposed and stopped.

After he was diagnosed with cancer, Wayne McLaren lobbied for tighter restrictions on advertising and even stood up at a shareholders meeting of Philip Morris to ask them then to back off on their advertising and marketing.

Did they listen?

The Earth as a casualty

We've become a society obsessed with quick fixes and cheap alternatives. But what is the cost? The cigarette, cup of coffee, hamburger and the new, cheap piece of furniture made from chipboard all give us pleasurable feelings (no matter how brief they may be) when we introduce them into our lives. This is my chance to spruik for the environment and only because I want to raise the awareness of what is going on beyond our backyards. I don't want you to feel guilty but I do want you to be aware of the problems so that you may take action.

Forests are being cut or burned down every day and the volume is reducing across the world not just because we are expanding in number as a race but because we consume more needless products. The people and governments of these countries realise there are profits to be made from consumerism and the land is exploited and cleared of natural vegetation to make way for cattle and cash crops.

Is the hamburger you just ate from a sustainable farm or from imported meat? Is the coffee you drank earlier from a rainforest alliance grower and supplier? Is the gold you are wearing from a mine that uses sound environmental practices? Does that cheap piece of furniture made from chipboard come from a sustainable local source or was it made from rainforest products and imported? Does that piece of chocolate you ate contain palm oil imported from overseas? Was the tobacco in the cigarettes you purchase grown in a local farm or was it imported from a developing country?

Your action is to be more aware of the power each person has to have an impact not just on the world directly around them but on the entire globe. By making better choices and perhaps by helping someone else to change their ways you can help just that little bit more.

I've harped on about the resources used so now it's time to turn to the litter created by smoking. With over 1 billion smokers worldwide and the average smoker having 30 cigarettes per day it would be fair to say there would be at least 30 billion cigarettes consumed *every day*.

Approximately 80 per cent of cigarettes currently produced have filters so that would equal 24 billion filtered cigarettes smoked and discarded each day across the world.

Does it make you wonder about the state of the world? Did you know that the white cotton-like material that forms the filter is generally a plastic fibre that can take up to 15 years to decompose? These plastic fibres are designed to be packed closely together and are hollow so that they can supposedly absorb and trap the vapours and smoke particles which become the brown 'tar' you can see at the end.

If these cigarette butts are designed to catch this material and there are billions of cigarette butts being thrown out of car windows, stubbed out on streets or disposed of in landfill then some consideration needs to be given to the poisoning of the land and waterways. These used butts contain a volume of 'tar' which has been proven as poisonous and certainly lethal. Butts that have remnants of tobacco attached have been shown to kill not just animals and sea creatures, but also very young children who have consumed the butts by mistake.

Think now about the state of the world's waterways. Were you aware that stormwater drains on the streets generally feed water directly out to the ocean or into waterways without treatment or filtering? Were you aware that the most prolific form of trash found in waterways and on beaches around the world is the seemingly innocuous cigarette butt? How often do you see people throwing butts out the window of their car?

It is not just about the butts either. Consider the production of butane for lighters and the CO_2 they give off when burned. Perhaps the 300 billion matches and the

200 billion matchbooks produced annually worldwide will get you thinking about the resources used.

I have not included these figures to make you feel guilty but to show you what the impact of the smoking pandemic is on the world and not just in terms of your own personal health.

Playing with fire

A very real and disturbing statistic associated with cigarettes is the high fire danger that a forgotten or improperly discarded cigarette causes. The incidence of death associated with fires ignited by cigarettes is as many as one in four—far more than any other single fire cause.

Contrary to popular belief the main victim base of deaths by cigarette-induced fires is generally not the smoker who falls asleep with a lit cigarette but innocent people in the proximity after a cigarette has been forgotten or improperly discarded.

Smouldering combustion is a slow process and operates at a lower temperature than an open flame. It can be sustained by many common materials such as wood, coal, cotton, polyurethane foam (as found in almost all sofas and lounges) and of course tobacco. You've seen smouldering in action every time you have lit up a cigarette and watched it slowly burn down. Instead of being in an open and gaseous phase the smouldering combustion works on the surface of the solid material.

The sequence of events in a deadly smouldering fire can begin with a lit cigarette being discarded on something like a couch. Here's how it can happen:

- The foam core heats up and begins to smoulder.

- The combustion slowly spreads to the interior of the cushion with the shell acting as a thermal insulator.

- The smouldering combustion continues undetected for a long period of time.

- Large amounts of heat, smoke and flammable poisonous gas are released.

- Heated gases (mostly carbon monoxide) fill the room or building and generally render any occupants of the room or building unconscious by fumes and smoke inhalation.

- The ambient temperature of the room and its contents increase towards flash point.

- The high volume of heated gas allows rapid combustion of the room and building when flash point is reached or an ignition source is applied.

Recently, after a month of researching fires and the effects, I had the good fortune to be passing a smouldering fire in a public rubbish bin while walking along a city street in Melbourne, Australia.

I was able to observe first-hand the smoke and the heat that was produced from the top of the trash container. On a dark street it was hard to notice unless you walked right past it. There was no telltale flame or glow of a normal fire; instead, there was just the heat emanating from the top and the acrid smoke. Looking around it was easy to see how this seemingly innocuous smouldering could have turned into a serious blaze. The large plastic bin was full of paper and was one of a row that awaited collection. There were cars parked within inches of the bins and so it goes on.

When the fire brigade arrived I was surprised to observe the sheer volume of water they used to ensure that the ignition source was extinguished. The fire fighter had to move the contents of the bin around to douse all of the smouldering material with water and completely extinguish the threat.

In a later interview with a retired fire investigator, I found the attitude towards the type of fire was interesting. If there is one thing that makes a fire fighter angry it is the fact that someone can cause mayhem and destruction through the simple act of ignorance of tossing a lit cigarette into a rubbish bin.

Let's now look beyond the problem of cigarettes on the world around you to the solution — your solution.

Chapter 4

SMOKING AND YOUR LIFE

The noblest pleasure is the joy of understanding.

Leonardo Da Vinci

I believe there are some perceived advantages to smoking that need to be discussed so you can change your present behaviour. You need to understand that these so-called benefits are not helping you and are culprits in keeping you comfortable within the circular pattern of behaviour in your life.

Perceived benefit: relaxation

The act of separating yourself from a task or situation can be restorative and can help calm your mind. Over time you have created a connection between this act and smoking so it will be only natural for your subconscious mind to ask you to reach for a cigarette. In stressful times it can be of benefit to disconnect from the situation (whether it is work or domestic) whereby you can take the time to find a clear solution or just take a break instead of perhaps adding fuel to a fire. In these times you will need to be consciously aware of your actions and you'll need to create a new and empowering relaxation program.

Take the time to breathe deeply and enjoy the invigorating feel of the fresh air as it enters deep into your lungs. Take a 'fresh air' break from now on.

Perceived benefit: camaraderie

The process of smoking allows people a chance to connect. This allows the cigarette to become associated with our basic human need for connection with others. The connection only has to be for the few minutes it takes to down a 'ciggie' and can fulfil a need to be a part of a group, chat or take one's mind off work for a short while.

You'll need to find other excuses to begin a conversation with others from now on when you step out for a 'fresh air break'.

How confident are you at initiating conversation with people you do not know?

....

....

What sort of effect will you have on a stranger's day when you politely greet them on the street with a kind word and a smile?

....

....

Could there be a flow-on effect caused by your kind action?

....

....

Perceived benefit: time away from work

Sometimes it feels good to step out of the building and away from your desk or wherever you spend eight, 10 or 16 hours a day. This again can be a de-stressor yet if something at work is creating problems for you then it may be time to tackle the problem in a more direct manner. Sometimes simple misunderstandings can blow out of proportion and can cause extra problems and friction.

The tedium of repetitive work can also be broken by the act of changing your behaviour for a few minutes.

Does your work have a counselling service or is there someone you can consult with to rectify a situation? Some workplaces have stressful factors every day so it may be up to you to create a more empowering coping mechanism, one that may better serve your true needs.

Consider that the average smoker takes six short breaks each day for a period of 10 minutes each. This equates to the loss of approximately five or six hours production time per week, per person. The financial crash of 2008 has illustrated how close businesses can come to collapse when hard times hit. It has highlighted the importance of job security, cash flow and productivity. By stopping smoking you may just be able to add a new level to the bottom line of the business which could lead to a new level of success for the business and for yourself. Going back to the idea of the accident chain, this is a chance for you to have a positive impact upon someone else's chain.

Needs versus wants

Distinguishing the difference between what you need and what you may want will change your whole life—from your health to your financial situation.

'Needs' and 'wants' are two very different thought processes.

The basic human needs include:

- shelter

- food

- water

- air

- sleep

- sex.

Maslow's hierarchy of needs shows the more complex needs of humans. They are:

- *safety and security*: our personal need to feel safe and comfortable

- *love and belonging:* our need for love and connection with others

- *self-esteem:* our need to believe and feel as though we are champions in our world

- *self-actualisation*: vitality, creativity, self-sufficiency, authenticity, playfulness, meaningfulness

- *peak experiences:* things that raise us to a new level, or that are exciting or invigorating.

What other needs do you feel you have that you can add to the list?

....

....

Learning to ask yourself and others the question 'Do you need that or do you want it?' may be the difference between getting what you desire or being a slave to an automatic subconscious program that will control you for the rest of your life.

Humans are brilliant electrochemical machines, possibly the most marvellous things on this earth. The complexity of multiple systems within systems with which we are created is unique and needs to be understood in order to move forwards. You can manage your electrical/chemical responses and impulses with clear and objective thinking, or you can let the responses control you. Eating chocolate creates an automatic chemical reaction in the brain akin to sexual pleasure. So, too, does buying wonderful new things, which is why sugar consumption and shopping can become, dare I say, 'addictive'.

The imbalance in the natural state of the human body caused by external stimulants creates a rollercoaster effect that can be difficult for the body to manage. Often when a stimulant is introduced, the body's own natural system can be retarded and even irreparably damaged. Over a period of time the requirement to boost the dose of the external stimulant can increase as the natural system slowly reduces its own production and shuts down. This is how the slippery slope of getting into a program of introducing external stimulants can begin and quickly result in a feeling of dependence.

You need to be in control of that particular electrochemical process if you are going to beat smoking.

Asking the question 'Do you need that or want it?' will interrupt that automatic response of pleasure. You will rationalise things a lot better and you will find it easier to distinguish the difference between your needs and wants.

The rational brain can interrupt the automatic running of programs by the subconscious mind. We all have different triggers and reactions but simply asking the 'want versus need' question will always bring you back to a level playing field and empower you to make the best decision.

Do you really *need* that cigarette or do you *want* it?

....

....

What do you *want* in your life?

....

....

What do you feel that you *need*?

....

....

Are you happy with your current position in the game of life?

....

....

I'm guessing you're not happy if you're reading this and there is something that you want to change. Write it down. What would you like to change?

....

....

If you had absolutely no limitations on resources, what would you change about your life right now?

....

....

What in your present life resembles your ideal life?

....

....

What are you happy with in your life right now?

....

....

What do you believe you are doing right that's working for you?

....

....

What are you doing or what beliefs do you have that are already moving you towards your goals?

....

....

How does that make you feel?

....

....

Have these questions helped to clarify what strengths you posses and what you need to be focusing on? If not, what else can you do? Who can you ask for assistance?

....

....

When you are in need of resources, where can you find them?

....

....

If the questions have helped, what else can you do to expand on your answers?

....

....

Making your current actions and the new actions clear and concise will help you to move forward at a better pace.

Show me the money

Have you ever calculated how much money you could save when you stop smoking?

Of course you have—I'm sure you are reminded every time you buy a packet over the counter.

Allow me to put it in perspective.

For the sake of this exercise I have averaged the price of a packet of cigarettes to US$10—about the average price of a packet of cigarettes around the world. (In Australia at the time of publication the price was up to A$17.50 per packet.)

Smoke a pack a day and it becomes a US$70 per week hit to your pocket (at US$10 per pack).

How many hours per week do you have to work to pay for those cigarettes with *after-tax* dollars?

Multiply 70 by 52 and you will be spending in the order of US$3500 *after-tax* dollars per year.

How hard are you working to pay for your cigarettes and how do you feel about that?

If you are making a basic wage, were you aware that you had to work for approximately two months per year to pay for your cigarettes?

Are you a slave to smoking?

What could you do or buy for US$3500 each year? Some examples:

- Buy two adult airfares to somewhere exotic?

- Get ahead on your mortgage repayments? How much would you save on your home loan in interest payments? How much sooner could you own your home?

- Pay the school tuition for your children?

- Pay out your credit card debts?

- Buy a new TV and entertainment unit?

- Buy a nice king size bed to help you sleep better?

- Start an investment account?

What would you like to do with your $3500 each year? Fill out your answer below.

....

....

How would you feel if you knew that you got out of bed each morning because you enjoyed your work and not because you had to work the whole day just to pay for your cigarettes?

An interesting concept by governments is to raise the tobacco taxes to discourage smoking. Interviewing smokers has shown me that this method does not work and only increases their financial burdens.

Considering the funds raised by governments from excise and taxes compared with the amount spent to treat and educate smokers, the extra tax revenue raised could be seen as just another money-making scheme.

A hypothetical situation

A person approaches you and offers you a choice of two options.

Option 1: You can have US$100000 cash there and then, no tax or fees and no waiting.

Option 2: You can have a single cent immediately. This single cent must be placed in an investment account where the balance doubles in value every day for a total of only 30 days.

One cent becomes two, then four, then eight, and so on.

Which would you choose?

Would you like to start a savings account and gain income from the interest?

Would you like to own a portfolio of properties that are not only producing an income for you but are also increasing in value with each year that passes?

What action can you take today to start learning how to invest?

Without altering your current lifestyle or living standards you could transfer the money previously spent on cigarettes directly into an investment. With the added leverage of the regular cash injection every week your investment could increase in strength and size very quickly.

Would you like to earn money through your investments without having to spend much of your precious time working for it?

Would you like to be able to take six weeks off from work without having to worry about where the money will come from to pay the bills?

The power of investing correctly is massive and can change the way you look at life. You can enjoy more interaction with your family and friends, you can help others, you can focus on what you like to do and you can create more 'time'.

A key with investing properly is education. Talk with people who are successfully involved in property development, property speculation, share market trading, foreign exchange trading, term deposit accounts or managed funds. Ask them to show you the right ways and methods to gain success.

Keep your eyes open for opportunities.

Were you aware that by stopping smoking you can reduce your life insurance premiums as you will become a 'lower risk' candidate? If you have life insurance then give your agent a call. This is just one of the ways you can create more cash flow in your life.

Now is a good time to use your new spare change to donate to charity. Giving money to a good cause not only helps others (and make you feel good) but it teaches you that there is more than enough in your budget to go around.

Your confidence will improve. You will start walking taller, smiling more and saying hello to strangers.

What kind of world might that produce for you?

What effect do you think you might have on other people's lives?

What do you think a smile and a kind word will do for a stranger's day?

Why bother counting the days?

Almost every smoker I encounter knows to the minute how long it has been since their last cigarette. Do not do this. Let it go. You do not need to reinforce a feeling of loss from your life. Counting the days implies to the brain that it is missing out on something.

In my eyes you either don't smoke or you do. Now, you don't. There are far better things to remember and keep count of than how many days it was since your last cigarette. Birthdays, holidays, pay days!

If someone asks you how long it has been reply, 'I feel better now that I don't smoke and I won't do it again, I have no need for it'. Then change the topic. How is work going? How is your partner? How are the kids? Did you catch the game on the weekend?

Changing the focus is a great way to continue forwards with ease and away from the old smoking program as it will become diluted and will lose its strength rapidly. If you catch yourself thinking about smoking again you can always use focus breaker that I will help you develop later. If you do it in front of someone else then I'm sure you will both get a good laugh out of your crazy behaviour.

Out of sight is definitely out of mind.

Out of mind is also out of mind.

Chapter 5

SMOKING AND YOUR BODY

To keep the body in good health is a duty...otherwise we shall not be able to keep our mind strong and clear.

Buddha

One of the biggest challenges smokers face is dealing with cravings. To crave something is to have a strong desire for it, perhaps even begging for it. What needs to happen for you to solve this problem for yourself is to consciously be aware of your thoughts and processes as you change the behaviour of smoking.

As the mind goes through the peak and turns to the downward section of the nicotine cycle (this commences within a few minutes) the body and mind begin to miss the sensation. The further down the slope the more the longing by the brain will increase. The brain begins to become dependent upon the introduction of the external stimulant and becomes lazy in producing its own 'feel good' products. This dependence creates the ups and downs of the 'cravings'.

The power of focused thought can have an amazing effect upon your actions. A problem people encounter when they stop smoking is they become fixated upon the loss of their cigarettes and the sensation of smoking. The more they fixate upon the loss, the stronger the desire becomes to have just one cigarette to alleviate what they are feeling. It is like adding fuel to a raging fire until they ultimately cave in to the temptation. This is a point where the focus needs to change from the cigarette and the desire to have one to a completely different subject.

Take a moment now to create a focus breaker. What can you do to change the focus of your thoughts? Can you make a funny face in the mirror, tweak your own nose like one of the Three Stooges or pinch the skin on the back of your hand?

My focus breaker is:

....

....

You'll notice that as soon as you break the focus of your thoughts and interrupt the fixation, you'll be able to switch your brain into a rational mode where you can reason with yourself and regain control of your impulses.

Be your own leader and command respect, engender loyalty, maintain your integrity and be responsible for your actions and behaviour. Congratulate yourself whenever you have a victory and be proud of your abilities.

Take a minute now to imagine how good you'll feel when your body is free from external stimulants and is back at its natural balance point.

Something you need to do in changing your pattern is change the language you use — the word 'craving' must go. A 'craving' manifests itself in your thoughts and can be hard to get rid of. Like an annoying jingle on television or on the radio, it just gets stuck in your head. The people who market products know the benefits and strengths of an effective jingle or catchphrase. This can be another aspect of the mind that we can employ to work for you instead of against you.

When you see someone smoking a cigarette you need to be aware that your subconscious mind will receive a signal from the old program it used to run on a regular basis. This signal needs to be interrupted and changed to something that will be of benefit to you. You'll need to stop that annoying jingle in your head before it consumes your thoughts.

Your focus breaker can be used to interrupt and change the signals. This will become easier as time passes.

Can you write down two experiences in the space provided where you felt strong feelings of warmth, excitement and happiness? Be sure to add plenty of details, including colours and feelings.

....

....

....

....

The above experiences will now become your conscious focal points for times when you may be feeling the urge to smoke, a sort of transcendental meditation to calm your mind. Use your focus breaker to initially take the smoking focus away and get the annoying jingle out of your head. It will go but it just may take a bit of effort on your part.

Oh, and remember to breathe.

The inside word—effects on your body

I originally wrote this section with the point in mind to provide some education on the physical problems that smoking can cause. I literally spent months writing pages of problems and symptoms using references from hundreds of pages of studies and research. One morning recently I woke up and realised I had to can the idea. Why? The book would have to be a 1000 pages long to allow fair and equal reference to each problem. Everything from peripheral vascular disease (PVD), macular degeneration in the eyes, periodontal disease, hearing loss and cancerous growths to back problems caused by the rapid contraction of muscles during coughing fits. Understanding the problems that smoking causes is an important piece in completing the puzzle but I certainly didn't want to bore you with too much detail.

During my revelation it dawned on me that we have a few simple operating systems that allow us to live and function. Impair one of these systems and these are bound to be flow-on effects that will transfer to every single operating system and cell in our body in at least one form.

We know smoking inhibits the body from absorbing its main fuel, oxygen. Carbon monoxide replaces the oxygen in the blood and the body simply cannot maintain its intended processes. This fuel starvation and the subsequent improper processing of waste products will affect us in different ways. Since there are an infinite number of processes in our bodies then the results of fuel starvation and improper waste disposal can, and will, have an effect upon every single system.

Scientists are spending a lot of money and time in researching health and smoking to come up with results that to me are obvious. It's what I have been telling my students for many years—rubbish in equals rubbish out. When introducing external toxins like cigarette smoke or atmospheric pollution into a system such as the human body it can be expected that every single process and system can potentially be affected in some form.

A common thread in all of the research papers is that they all conclude by saying the best way to heal is to stop smoking.

The body can repair itself so if you want to feel amazing, look younger, have more passion, enjoy better sex and love your life then now is your time.

Make a list below of the specific areas of your health that you would like to see improvements in.

I would like to see improvements in:

....

....

The inside word—lungs and respiration

The lungs are made of many millions of tiny sacs that allow the oxygen that is breathed in to be absorbed into the blood system. The introduction of chemicals and carbon monoxide means that the sacs are absorbing the wrong materials into the bloodstream and less of the right stuff.

The 'tar' contained in the cigarette smoke blocks these sacs and the hot smoke also damages the lungs and can kill them off. This blocking and damage obviously makes it harder for the body to absorb oxygen. This lack of clean fuel and introduction of toxins means that the body's normal operating procedures, defence and healing mechanisms will be impaired.

Our bodies are a complex array of systems working together. Throw in toxins like alcohol, drugs or cigarettes and they will negatively affect our physiology on some level. The toxins might send signals that our brains interpret as 'feeling good' but the changes in the electrical and chemical messages are only fooling our bodies and minds.

The respiration process not only lets the oxygen in but also allows the body to release carbon dioxide which is a waste product of our bodies' cells. Under normal conditions our bodies are processing average levels of carbon dioxide but a smoker's body has to process far greater levels than normal along with other toxins such as the poisonous carbon monoxide. The negative compounding effect of smoking on the body is a factor in the accumulation of poisons which can cause irregularities such as chronic disease and cancerous growths.

Stopping smoking will allow your lung capacity to increase, and your lungs to start working properly and process oxygen a lot better.

Depending on how long you have been smoking and what you physically do on a daily basis your lungs will need some time to recover. Unfortunately, owing to their makeup they will never recover fully but they will improve. You may initially develop a nasty cough that will result in off-colour mucus coming from your lungs. This coughing is perfectly normal as it is the body's method of cleansing the lungs and will be more prevalent in the morning because of the settling effect during sleep. Explain your cough to those around you so they understand what is happening with your body. The cough will disappear over a relatively short period of time as the body expels the buildup. This can range from a couple of days to a few weeks.

Do you feel out of breath on occasion?

Do you already have a nasty cough in the morning?

Have you attributed that cough to your smoking or do you blame it on something else?

Do you find that you sneeze for no apparent reason?

How much would you like to wake up tomorrow morning and feel like a million dollars?

The inside word—the lymphatic system

The lymphatics contain and transport lymph which is a clear water-like fluid. It is a system of small vessels that permeates nearly every part of the body that contains blood vessels. Lymphatics are known as absorbents because of their ability to absorb certain materials from the tissues and bring them into the circulation—a sort of biological waste disposal system on the tiniest level imaginable. The lymph nodes and other associated organs serve to filter the lymph to remove any microorganisms or particles and act as our body's system for fighting infection. Lymph nodes can be good indicators of infection in the body as they can swell and become sore. If you've been sick in the past you might recall the doctor checking the side of your neck, your armpit or the condition of your tonsils.

This system can handle a regular amount of work but as with anything if it is placed under excess stress then problems can occur. It is this basic cellular 'house cleaning' where smoking has its effects and problems. The chemicals present in cigarettes and the nicotine cause this system to be constricted and not function as it should. If the removal of toxins and effective fighting of infection cannot take place then it is only a matter of time before adverse effects could be expected.

Have you tried any detox diets in the past?

Stopping smoking will be the best detox ever with no expensive and potentially dangerous fad dieting.

The inside word—blood and the circulatory system

There is no chance of our bodies working without blood. It is a fuel and filtration system we require. The average adult body has approximately four to six litres of blood. One purpose of blood is to carry oxygen around the body. Now, if a main purpose of the lungs is to introduce the oxygen to the blood and smoking directly affects the lungs' ability to do their job, how do you think this might affect your circulatory system? Will you have premium fuel or dirty, sludgy fuel going through your circulatory system? How do think your engine is running right now?

Blood gets its red colour from the oxygen reacting with the haemoglobin. The more oxygen in the blood, the redder it will appear. The act of smoking decreases the level of oxygen in the blood and increases the level of poisonous carbon monoxide and toxins so the blood of a smoker may appear darker and more viscous than normal. Think back now to when you last cut yourself—did you bleed?

I recently witnessed a chronic smoker receive a very deep cut on the back of her hand. The normal process would have been for her hand to bleed openly to allow the body to cleanse the cut and then for the blood to begin coagulating and clot so the repair process may begin. Her skin opened up but did not bleed, it didn't even appear red. Her circulatory system is obviously not working to its optimum and is actually at a point where it could be considered dangerous. The chemicals present in cigarette smoke cause the blood to become thick and sticky and to clot more easily. This danger becomes vividly apparent when the smoker is on the operating table during surgery. The impaired healing process also highlights the fact that smokers have higher rates of complications and failure during surgery and also take longer to recover than people who don't smoke. Scarring can also be more prominent in a smoker compared with normal healthy scarring because of the impaired repair process.

White blood cells are the fighters of infection but without correct blood flow it becomes harder for the body to combat infections and problems. This opens the body up in another way to attack and complications. Give some thought to your inner workings and consider what is happening. Take the time now to listen to your body and see what it is telling you. Close your eyes and feel your heart beating in your chest.

Can you feel your fingertips pulsing as your heart beats?

Can you feel the warmth flood over your body as the blood is pumped by your heart through your arteries?

Have you had chest pains or unexplainable pain your arms?

Have you felt short of breath?

Can you make it up a flight of stairs without having to stop or slow down?

Do you get pain or 'pins and needles' in your toes and feet?

How would you rate your sex life?

By stopping smoking you will experience improvements not just in every day functioning but also in your sex life. This is partly due to the fact that blood flow to all of the extremities and genitals will improve as the body cleans itself out and returns to a state of normality. It's painfully obvious to me that a cleaner running system should allow for everything about your body to improve.

Male smokers who have previously experienced erectile dysfunction should see an improvement in their ability to achieve and maintain an erection as well as see increases in their fertility, desire and libido.

Females who stop smoking should also experience an increase in sexual sensation and fertility as well as a stabilising and possible decrease in menstrual pain and duration after stopping smoking. It has been shown statistically that females who smoke are more likely to reach menopause at a lower than average age.

The implications of smoking on the female's circulatory system are massive not only for themselves but also their unborn child. Irregularities such as pregnancy difficulties, birthing problems and deformities of the foetus occur because of the quality of the 'fuel' that is supplied to the baby and the pregnant mother's impaired bodily systems.

Experiment: your circulatory system

This is a simple experiment to test your circulatory system.

Does the colour return to your fingernail after you compress it? Try it now.

Pinch the tip of your finger and watch the full colour of your nail return. How long does it take?

(Note: if it's cold then more of your blood will be inside your torso than in your extremities so it will be natural for it to take longer for the colour to return.)

A healthy person with good circulation should note that the fingernail will return its colour almost immediately. What did you observe?

Skin care

Skin is the largest organ of the human body. I think that most of us forget that skin has two sides—there is the external stuff we see, but skin also has inner layers we need to consider.

The skin is very dynamic as it is constantly regenerating and repairing, as well as protecting us from external elements. In order to repair and regenerate the skin relies upon oxygen and nutrients supplied to it by small blood vessels. One of the direct symptoms of nicotine use is the constriction of blood vessels. This constriction will directly affect the supply of nutrients and oxygen to skin cells. You can apply a vast amount of the most expensive skin creams to the outside of your skin but it will only still be doing half the job.

The effects of smoking on the skin show as:

- premature wrinkling and sagging from a reduction in the elastin and collagen levels

- dryness and discoloration in the skin which especially affects the face and the fingers of a smoker caused by the direct application of heat and smoke

- wrinkling around the lips of the smoker caused by the pursing of the lips when drawing back

- wrinkling around the eyes caused by the squinting when smoke enters the eyes.

The start of a good skin care regime actually begins with stopping smoking. The elasticity of your skin should improve as oxygen levels increase and the skin regains its natural elastin and collagen levels.

Our bodies are the most amazing machines and I'm constantly in awe of how our systems evolved and how things work. Watch a Formula One team in action and you'll see some of the world's best mechanics, engineers, drivers and designers at work. These ultimate racing cars get treated with the utmost respect, not just because they cost so much, but because the engineering is so precise in every single aspect that one small change upsets the balance. The engine from a Formula One car generally is completely rebuilt after one race and is basically redundant after the season. One year from start to finish.

Our bodies are meant to last for over 75 years. We don't have a warranty or a refund policy and although we can now get a 'cut and polish' or a few dents removed through plastic surgery, if we damage our bodies they do not get replaced. Our bodies are a heck of a lot more important than an F1 car.

Why then do so many people treat them like pieces of junk with the food and chemicals they burden them with? What can you do today to begin caring for your skin and your body so you can look and feel younger?

Sleep

We sleep for approximately 30 per cent of our lives so let's pay sleep some respect and attention. We tend to spend a lot of money on cars, stereos and televisions yet we don't give much thought to investing in the right bases, mattresses, pillows or bedding. Unfortunately, when we go to buy a bed or bedding we are generally purchasing from stores where the people aren't trained in the art of correct sleep and most consumers are unfortunately motivated by the lowest price alone. Injuries, excess stress, incorrect pillows and bedding, unsatisfactory mattresses and other outside influences can adversely affect sleep quality. Smoking is also a real culprit in creating sleep disturbances.

There are six different stages of sleep:

- *Stage 1:* a period of light sleep and a time where people drift in and out of sleep. Many people can experience muscle contractions followed by a sense of falling.

- *Stage 2:* in this stage eye movement stops and brainwaves slow down with possible intermittent bursts of rapid brain activity.

- *Stage 3:* brainwaves are predominantly slower and in the delta region.

- *Stage 4:* brainwaves are almost exclusively delta waves and it is in stages 3 and 4 that we are said to be in deep sleep. This is the repair stage.

- *Stage 5:* REM phase. This is another phase of deep sleep where breathing becomes rapid, irregular and shallow. The heart rate and blood pressure rise and this is where the eyes move rapidly and people experience dreams.

- *Waking.*

Smokers generally find it harder to fall asleep than non-smokers and also stir from sleep more during the night. Since nicotine causes the constriction of blood vessels, increases blood pressure and interrupts the central nervous system, it's easy to see why a smoker will find it harder to get proper rest. The body repairs and rebuilds its systems during the deep sleep phase. When the sleep process is interrupted and the body wakes up prematurely, it has to recommence the sleep cycle beginning from Stage 1. The smoker therefore spends less time in the deep sleep phase and misses out on the restorative and repair effects naturally provided by the body.

You will need to expect that you may initially experience more disturbances in your sleep patterns now that you've stopped smoking because your body will be working to find its natural balancing point. If you have made a conscious decision to stop smoking, I believe you should have the best night's rest tonight than you have experienced in a long time.

If you have been sleeping badly then your body may want to shut down during the day. If you feel the need for a nap then do so if you can. See if you can nap for at least an hour for the rest to be at least partially effective but try not to let it affect your normal sleeping patterns.

Nicotine withdrawal has been documented as producing symptoms which include irritability, restlessness, anxiety and a craving for nicotine. Interestingly enough, the symptoms (except for the nicotine factor) also sound like what may be encountered by a person suffering from a lack of quality sleep.

With the sleeping disturbances can come higher levels of irritation and intolerance which may affect other people in your life. It's important to take responsibility for your behaviour and actions and let people know what you are going through. This way they can be more supportive and prepared. The key here is the word 'may'. You may experience this. I have spoken to a lot of non-smokers who have felt no ill effects whatsoever, just an amazing feeling of ease.

Be sure to recognise the stages you are experiencing and through heightened awareness you will be able to create ways to manage with the changes this may bring. Provided you have no injuries or conditions that affect your sleep you will soon be enjoying the proper rest that your 'healing machine' needs to repair and rebuild each night.

You will feel your energy levels increase, your memory will improve and your ability to focus and concentrate will improve. With improved sleep will come a vast improvement in your quality of life!

Does the prospect of an improved quality of life excite you?

....

....

How do you think you will feel when you get a great night's sleep on a regular basis?

....

....

How will you benefit from a better night's sleep?

....

....

Are you looking forward to a great night of sleep tonight? Do you desire the best night of restful sleep you have ever had and to do the same again tomorrow night?

....

....

What would you like to do when you first wake up tomorrow morning?

....

....

Here are some tips to help you sleep well:

- Have a quick, warm shower about an hour before you go to bed. This will help to relax your muscles and quiet your mind. The steam will also have a cleansing effect on your lungs.

- Read a book or flick through a magazine. Working on the computer or playing computer games might be physically inactive but the stresses on your mind and eyes mean that your mind will still be running when you are trying to fall asleep.

- Avoid coffee or stimulants after 4 pm.

- Avoid eating after 7 pm so that your body is not processing food when it should be approaching the rest phase.

- Perform some stretches and loosen the muscles up. This can assist the muscles during the repair period of sleep and help you wake up feeling physically fit the next day.

- Take five minutes to quiet your mind. Perform some deep breathing and think only of the breath going in and out. Use this time to focus on your body and feel where you may be holding tension. Note how your muscles are when you breathe deeply. Do you feel tension in your neck or shoulders? Do you feel tension in your lower back? Are you holding the muscles of your gut tense and are you able to breathe deeply and effectively? Use the deep breathing to release this tension and relax your muscles—in doing so you'll find that a comfortable and restful sleep ensues.

- Play some calming music instead of watching television.

- Turn the lights down in your house towards bedtime. The darkening of the area will settle your mind and prepare you for sleep.

- Take some time to talk and connect with the people around you to resolve any issues or get things off your mind. This will help you get to sleep without your mind racing.

- Write your thoughts or ideas down on a notepad so your mind can be calm and clear for sleep preparation.

Here are some tips on how to wake up well:

- When you wake up you need to get straight out of bed instead of pressing the 'snooze' button.

- Get excited about the morning and what you have in store for the day ahead—it's a great way to start the day.

- Say the following sentence and follow it up. 'I am excited about today because …'

- Be grateful for a wonderful night's rest and the opportunity to enjoy another day.

- Instead of an external stimulant to start your day, try an internal one—put on a smile.

- If you wake up with thoughts racing in your head, write them down.

- Have a glass of water beside the bed that you can drink in its entirety as soon as you get out of bed. You have just fasted for eight hours and your body will appreciate the fluid.

Passive smoking

Passive smoking is a real problem and with the recognition of the dangers has come lobbying for new government legislation to support the general public. Smoking is fine if the smoker's decision does not affect others' rights to breathe fresh air. In Australia, smoking has been banned in nightclubs, hotels, public buildings and restaurants, as well as in cars with children as passengers. This is great for reducing the incidences of passive smoking.

Unfiltered cigarette smoke in the open air can greatly affect the non-smoker, especially young children who are in a confined space with a smoker. The development of their lungs can be affected and can result in respiratory problems such as asthma.

To see the impact your smoking has had on people around you, try the following test.

The windscreen test

This exercise will take about five minutes for you to perform. Only do this if you smoke in your car.

Grab a tissue or two and go out to your car.

Note the opacity of the glass in front of your face.

Does it appear clear or greasy/filmy?

Take your tissue and wipe the glass in front of your face.

Be sure to write your findings down.

What colour is the gunk on the tissue?

Have a close look and note the consistency of the gunk.

Is it a dark, sticky, yellow–brown colour?

What do you think of it?

How does it make you feel to see that on the tissue?

Do you have children or pets and have you smoked in the car with them?

Have you smoked in an apartment or house with people you love inside?

Have an objective look at the paint of the ceiling above your favourite seat— is it still white?

The alternatives to nicotine

Are the alternatives to nicotine doing you any good? If nicotine is such an addictive drug and you want to stop smoking then why would you substitute one form of nicotine for another?

It is an attempt to change the program by dilution but the product is still the same and can become a circular pattern of exchanging one thing for another. The substitution method is also designed as a reduction method wherein you gradually reduce the amount of nicotine absorbed on a daily basis.

Eventually, a lot of people who use substitutes and don't deal directly with the controlling program invariably end up just having one cigarette for old times' sake or as a test to see if the pill or patch worked. This will not happen to you.

Were you aware that most of the pharmaceutical companies that produce pills, patches and gums are owned by tobacco companies?

The idea of being in business is to make a profit and since people have begun to stop smoking in larger numbers, the tobacco giants have realised they can still make money from you by buying into businesses that smokers tend to turn to as an alternative — gum, patches and snack foods.

What substitute method have you tried in the past that perhaps didn't work for you?

....

....

What can you learn from what you have tried in the past?

....

....

What is your motivation to stop smoking today? Why are you reading this book right now?

....

....

The different methods are designed to assist people to reduce their behaviour one step at a time but what is often found with smokers is a belief that the method alone is what will cause them to stop. Some people create the incomplete belief of 'by using this patch I will stop smoking' or 'this pill will make me stop'. It's not the patch, gum or the pill that stops you from smoking—it will be the decision and resulting action ... it's ultimately up to you.

Going back to the accident chain theory, your personal chain can sometimes be broken by what I call 'Ah-ha' moments, things like being medically diagnosed with cancer or emphysema, but more often than not it will need to be broken by studying all of the available evidence, connecting with the material, coming to a decision and then consciously acting on it.

I am a believer in empowering people through knowledge. You then will make informed decisions to make the positive changes required. You will be able to regain control of your subconscious mind.

Your subconscious mind is fooled by the false 'pleasure' nicotine provides and the act of smoking creates. The chemical infatuation masks the real underlying issues and sensations.

Going 'cold turkey'

'Cold turkey' was a phrase coined by doctors observing heroin addicts as they suffered withdrawals. The blood moves towards the vital organs leaving the skin pallid and covered in 'goose bumps', making the addict's skin look like a turkey after it has been plucked and prepared. The brain interprets that lack of the 'feel good' substance as an attack on the body and so it reverts to a very basic primal survival mode.

The body and mind become used to the external stimulants and so the natural processes become impaired and slow down. When the body feels as though it is missing something it will send a message to the brain to ask it for more.

When you are hungry your brain receives a message and so the process begins of hunting for some food.

When you are thirsty the brain sends out the message that you need a drink of water.

When you have stopped smoking for a while the brain will receive the signal that there is no nicotine and so it will send out a message for you to take action. You can consciously interrupt this message and re-channel it to another area. The body will become confused for a short period of time until it learns that it has to recommence the production of its own 'feel good' products.

The language of stopping 'cold turkey' can falsely translate as a painful and sometimes dangerous method to engage in and so the brain shies away from taking action, preferring instead to retract into its comfort zone — smoking. It's only natural most of us will shy away from pain, discomfort or a fear of the unknown. When talking about stopping smoking and going 'cold turkey' with a smoker it is easy to see why there is not much enthusiasm for this method. And I agree with them.

You will not need to go 'cold turkey' and can leave that term behind you right now.

You will stop smoking in a positive and healthy way.

You are a person with sound judgement. You are a powerful individual who has made a choice based on good, clear thinking and planning to stop a program that had a negative impact on you and those around you.

The weight gain factor

One of the most debilitating excuses for not going ahead with stopping smoking is that of possible weight gain. This is one of the most common misconceptions of stopping smoking, so let's tackle it now.

If done correctly, stopping smoking does not have to have any affect on a person's weight. If anything the mind and body will be working more efficiently and a person's weight will decrease.

Would you say that you are at a healthy weight for your height right now? Are you in proportion for your body shape and type?

....

....

Do you feel as though you could lose some excess weight?

....

....

Smoking can serve as a dietary suppressant as it causes the body to 'clam up'. The body does not process the fuel in the correct manner. When people stop smoking the circulatory system will clean itself out and the fuel demands will increase. The right fuel is important because your body is going to be working hard to find its natural balance again.

Give some consideration to what you are eating. The mind has been fooled for so long by this external stimulant it may be easy to misinterpret the signals and turn to sugary or fatty foods to satisfy the old 'feel good sensation'. You do not need to do this. Were you aware that tobacco companies own some of the largest snack food brands in the world?

With the people that I have coached through the program I've found that weight loss is inevitable. Each person has found a new empowering program of health care and healthy eating to replace the smoking program. Your taste buds will kick in and you'll be keen to explore new flavours and even savour the food you regularly enjoy. Some foods high in sugars and fats taste good and are hard to resist but you need to pay attention to how your body feels after you eat unhealthy meals or snacks. You'll need to maintain your focus on your goals.

Do you feel bloated and uncomfortable or does your stomach do sideways flips and turns after eating a burger and chips? Do you feel tired to the bone and lethargic after eating fatty or sugary foods?

I certainly don't believe in denying yourself any pleasure as long as it is good for you and good for others. If you feel as though you deserve a reward for eating healthy food for a week then go ahead and have some chocolate or buy a burger. Savour the taste and textures and your brain will create a 'reward' link.

Do you feel good after you have eaten 'junk' food? Does your body feel as though it is processing the junk food in the correct manner?

You can still eat what you want as long as you balance out your intake of fuel and listen to your body. The harder you listen, the louder the benefits will be. I really enjoy the feeling after eating a delicious salad when my body tingles and all of the cells are shouting 'thank you'.

Think about the local farmers and their families you are supporting with your new eating habits. You are no longer supporting global companies that produce tobacco, snack food and pharmaceuticals. Doesn't it feel good?

Avoiding weight gain is going to take some work but you'll feel great and you'll enjoy the process. Would you rather feel bloated and lethargic sitting on the couch in front of the television or would you rather be outside doing something active after a good meal?

Find out what works for you and rediscover what you enjoy doing. This will involve creating new programs of getting outside and doing something physical regularly. Eating the proper foods and creating opportunities like parking further from the entrance to the shopping mall, taking the stairs or going for an evening walk after dinner will go a long way to creating a better quality of life for you.

With so much information about weight and weight loss out there a few things need to be clarified.

The human body and weight gain or loss can be broken into some simple general equations:

- More food in and less effort out = weight gain.

- Less food in and more effort out = weight loss.

- Balanced food plus balanced effort = weight management.

Do you believe you are close to or at your target weight?

....

....

What do you think having a better diet and increasing your movement will do for your health and your shape or size?

....

....

Do you think you are carrying excess fat on your body?

....

....

If you're carrying any excess fat then the chances for health problems increase. If you've been smoking for many years then it's a sure thing that you'll notice the following changes in how you feel as soon as you stop:

- You'll feel more energetic due to your blood and bodily systems cleaning themselves out and running more efficiently.

- You'll feel balanced as your systems equalise and operate as they should.

If you are planning to work with weights to build your strength, be aware muscle is denser and weighs more than fat. As you work out you'll remove fat but add muscle and so the scales may give you a confusing message. This is where using the *'feel'* test to plot your progress is usually a better option than using scales or standing in front of a mirror. Remember that a watched kettle never boils so perform the mirror test or use scales only once a month to give a positive interval between tests. Something you can monitor every day is your energy level and feeling of vitality. Your daily energy levels will increase incredibly over the first few weeks.

Ask yourself the question 'How do I feel?'

Do you feel as though you are off the couch and are getting more done in your day?

Do you feel as though you are interacting more with the people around you?

For years you have been orally fixated, performing a program of lifting your hand to your mouth and placing something in your mouth, often several times within a minute. It is this program that will result in weight gain if you replace the cigarette with food. Some people replace smoking with snacking often with sugar or fatty foods. Snacking can be all right to maintain your blood sugar levels and energy but the snacks need to be healthy. It is common for people to reach for chocolate, crisps or sweet biscuits when they feel that they need a 'lift'. It might explain why the tobacco companies have branched out to own snack food companies.

If you analyse your accident chain you will notice that the hand-to-mouth fixation has created regular links all the way through. Awareness of the program is the first key to stopping it. Your are now aware and you now have the power to consciously change the old pattern and break the chain. Finding something else to do with your hands will be important.

There are methods of stopping smoking that involve the use of placebo cigarettes or inhaler type machines. These methods change the inhalation of the chemicals into the system but some still deliver the nicotine the smoker still thinks they need and they continue to encourage the hand-to-mouth program.

Awareness of the hand-to-mouth program will help you to reduce the effects and with a bit of practice you will eliminate it.

When you catch yourself placing food or pens and pencils in your mouth you will need to break the program right there and take it out of your mouth. When you do this take a moment to listen to the signals your brain is trying to interpret. It would be a good time to stop what you are doing and have a glass of cold water to refresh and rehydrate. The instant relief to your system may be just what you need.

The art of eating properly

We all know about eating the right sorts of food so this isn't going to be a lesson on nutrition. This section is about the art of correct digestion processes. You might be wondering why I am including this in a book about smoking. Well, smoking places a lot of stress on the body as does incorrect digestion. I've included this to help you reduce any unnecessary stress on your body.

When I shared lunch with a successful Indian chef he observed the way I ate and offered some suggestions that have changed my life. I used to be like a wolf when I ate and tended to eat as fast as I could. For some reason my perception was that the faster I ate the more I would enjoy my food. It probably came from when I was young when it meant I could get to the dessert faster.

The process of digesting food begins with the mouth. The teeth reduce the large pieces of food and saliva gets introduced into the mix. It is the gastronomic art of chewing and enjoying our food that many of us are missing out on. The Buddhists call it mindful action or mindful eating.

I know that my mother told me to chew my food 50 times before swallowing but I never understood the reason why. The chef shared the reason. The more we chew our food and mix saliva means our stomach and intestines have less work to do in processing which allows more effective and efficient extraction of the nutrients.

This decrease in the work done by the body means that the energy saved can be transferred to more worthwhile pursuits.

I can honestly tell you that since I have been chewing my food more I feel so much better after eating. Instead of feeling heavy and bloated I feel alive and refuelled. I feel energised by the food I eat instead of being a victim of it.

Also, by chewing and processing my food properly I have observed that I am eating less than I was previously, almost by half.

This is also where the art of saying no comes in to play as well. It is not bad to leave a portion of your meal uneaten. The person who served you will not take it as an insult if you don't completely finish a meal.

By reducing my meal sizes I'm:

- saving money because I'm eating less

- able to maintain my weight easily

- able to enjoy a meal in its entirety

- able to enjoy the taste and the sensations provided by the different foods

- working out what a correct portion size of food should be so waste is kept to a minimum

- reducing the stress on my body

- feeling better after meals — I don't get stomach aches or that 'bloated' feeling

- feeling more energetic after meals and through the day

- not getting the ups and downs of energy through the day — my body is more balanced.

Talking about health and fitness

The human body is a complex mixture of electrical and chemical systems. Maintaining balance in these systems is important in maintaining a quality of life for you and for the people around you. For too long smoking has thrown out your natural balance so you're going to need to find it again.

It is only recently that humans have become more sedentary. In the Stone Age we hunted, gathered, fended for ourselves and had to run away from giant man-eating creatures. In the age of farming we worked the land, walked everywhere, built and repaired everything and bartered with others. They were times when humans were more active and 'out and about'. The Industrial Age brought in factories and inventions such as the 'production line'. The Information Age has brought automation and computers into our lives where we can now get everything done for us without leaving the comfort of our lounge rooms. Almost everything has become disposable.

This 'easing' of our lives has resulted in an explosion of obesity. People in developed countries are fast becoming overweight, undernourished (even though food is plentiful) and underexercised. It's time to get up and do something for yourself and for your family.

Every day we are bombarded with images on television and billboards that promote products that aren't good for us. From 'on the spot finance' to food products that contain more preservatives and sugars than they do natural products. Okay, yes, sugar is a natural product but the over-refined and processed stuff that we are fed is not doing much good. It's time to turn back to fresh vegetables, fruits, seafood, meats, grains and dairy products. It takes the same time to prepare a bowl of rice, vegetables and a stir-through sauce as it does to drive to the local take-away and back. When you listen to your body it is interesting hearing the big 'thank you' your body says when you eat some delicious vegetables.

Eating well is a main part in losing excess weight or maintaining a healthy balance. There are so many ways to prepare a healthy meal and make good food exciting and delicious. The cost benefits are massive, too, as eating properly means you will not be paying for fad diet products or unnecessary dietary supplements.

Eating more vegetables and fresh foods means regular trips to the local shops and may be a good chance for you to discover local suppliers of quality fresh foods such as butchers and greengrocers. Local farmers' markets can provide an exciting and stimulating source of entertainment versus hours spent sitting on the couch watching television. The good stores and markets should also be able to provide you with tips on food preparation, recipes, and hints on cooking.

How happy and energetic will you feel when you are eating well?

....

....

What will you do when you have more energy and stamina?

....

....

How will your life change when you are concentrating and remembering more?

....

....

After you have eaten well for a whole week how do you believe your body will feel? Would you feel lethargic?

....

....

How do you think you will feel after you have been eating well for a whole year?

....

....

What would you like to eat when your senses of taste and smell return?

....

....

Would you like to lose weight and gain a high level of fitness?

....

....

You don't have to go to a gym to get fit. In fact, you don't even have to move to exercise your muscles. While you're sitting there I want to illustrate what I mean so that you can create a link to exercising absolutely anywhere at any time.

Can you flex your thighs while you sit there?

Can you tense the muscles in your arm?

See if you can activate your abdominals (your stomach muscles), flex them and hold the flex for a couple of seconds and then relax. You can do this by sitting tall and using your muscles to pull your belly button towards your spine.

Can you now flex your chest muscles without moving? Of course you can, just switch your focus to your chest muscles and flex them.

Now try to flex your muscles at full strength.

Can you flex the same muscles at only half-strength?

It might take some practice to isolate the muscle groups but after a short period of time you'll find that your new-found body awareness will result in improvements in:

- posture

- circulation

- stress release

- focus

- self-awareness.

Focus is the key and it can work for any muscle group you wish. Performing these isometric contractions is a great way to relax your muscles before you go to sleep. You can lie in bed and flex each muscle group individually. Hold the tension for a few seconds and then release the muscles and relax. You can do this all the way from your toes to your face and head. In doing so you can discover areas of your body where you may be feeling and storing excess tension. This flexing of the muscles promotes the flow of oxygen throughout your body and opens up all of the pathways for the restorative effects of sleep to take place.

There are a few points to be aware of when exercising in general:

- Ask for help from a professional.

- Know what you would like to achieve from your workout. Is it strength, stamina, weight loss, flexibility or a combination?

- Warm up before you begin so that you don't pull a muscle or strain a tendon and injure yourself.

- Balance left and right, top and bottom, front and back.

- Work larger muscle groups first.

- Listen to your body and observe the results. Is what you are doing working for you?

- Maintain focus.

- Increase your range of motion and flexibility. The body has many joints designed to move in different ways. In working with a professional trainer you can discover your body's full range of motion and so can more effectively exercise the muscles. You can also be aware of safe ways to exercise muscles around complex joints like the hips and shoulders.

- Ensure you have variety in your exercise regime.

- Warm down after you have exercised.

- Enjoy a healthy balanced diet and feel your energy increase.

You can go for a walk around the block and admire the gardens—take your partner, take the dog. Be sure to say hello to other people who are out for a walk and take the time to compliment someone's efforts if you see them working in their garden.

Working out what you want to achieve from your workouts will give you an insight into how you should structure your plan.

You can engage the services of a professional who will be happy to create a program for you at your local gym. Also consider other options, including swimming, walking groups, martial arts, fitness groups in the park and local community centres.

What would you like to do or try?

Have you ever wanted to learn karate, tae kwon do or one of the many other martial arts? Perhaps something like tai chi, meditation or yoga would be more your style.

Would you like to go bushwalking or rock-climbing?

Do you and the dog need to go for a walk around the block?

Can you go and kick the football in the backyard or play some basketball in the playground down the street?

Could you walk to the local shopping centre for your groceries instead of driving?

Can you play a game of 'chasey' with the children?

Getting to the gym is good and if you can meet with friends or take a family member then motivation to get there will be easy. Perhaps you will make some new friends and find more enjoyment and fun entering your life. Is there a gym close by that you can walk or ride your bike to?

Every little bit of exercise is going to help and every second you spend off the couch is going to be a gift to yourself and to others.

Would you like to feel refreshed and energised after a walk along the beach or through the leafy paths of your local botanical gardens?

Where would you like to visit outdoors when your sense of smell returns to its full potential?

How much would you like to look in the mirror and see yourself carrying less weight?

How great do you think you will feel when you are fit and healthy?

What can you start doing today towards reducing your weight and increasing your fitness and freedom?

....

....

The key with your body and your mind is 'use it or lose it'.

Excuses, excuses

Excuses can be a quick way to release a level of responsibility or procrastinate. By using an excuse you can transfer the responsibility to something that is seemingly out of your control. Now you will regain your control and power over the world around you. This book has been designed as a comprehensive decision-making process and so we will work to eliminate all of the possible sources for excuses in regards to your stopping smoking today.

Think about the excuses you might have used in the past to avoid giving up smoking: 'Things are stressful and my cigarettes help me to cope'; 'I have run out of time today so I will try to stop smoking tomorrow'; 'With Christmas coming up, the kids have their school play, the car needs to be serviced, I need to prepare dinner and I'm tired so I don't have the time or energy to think about stopping smoking'.

One of the best excuses I ever heard was a friend of mine in high school who hadn't done his homework. He told the teacher that his mother had put his books in the microwave and cooked them by mistake! He was granted an extension just because the excuse was so ridiculous.

What are some of the excuses you have used in the past? Write them down now and let them go.

....

....

Excuses are a transfer of blame or responsibility. Using an excuse is easy to do and can make your life seem easier. But what does transferring the responsibility do?

Excuses disempower you.

Excuses are a delaying tactic and sometimes the delay is indefinite. One thing I teach people about excuses is that no-one else cares about why something hasn't been done. What they care about is what it means to them. An excuse may help someone become comfortable with the delay but it serves no real purpose. Eliminate the use of excuses from your repertoire. We all make mistakes so accept them, take ownership of your mistakes, learn from them and keep moving forwards.

Have you tried to become a non-smoker in the past?

What excuse did you tell yourself when you had another cigarette?

....

....

By writing down your excuses you are permanently removing them from your inner library.

This is where they will stay as you'll have no further use for them. Your excuses are gone.

If you are ready to become a non-smoker then getting rid of any excuses will play an important part in making your transition easier.

Ditch the excuses and take full responsibility for your actions. It's okay, just write them down and get rid of them. No-one else has to see them.

Chapter 6

YOUR FUTURE

Decide carefully, exactly what you want in life, then work like mad to make sure you get it!

Hector Crawford (1913–1991)

Throughout this book I have shared with you important knowledge that will assist you in your decision-making process towards successfully stopping smoking. When making a life change like stopping smoking you will create gaps in your regular programs of behaviour. Like water flowing back into a hollow, your smoking behaviour may want to return and there will be times when you unconsciously revert to the old patterns. Your awareness of this will help you to stop it from going too far and lighting up a cigarette. When your conscious mind kicks back in you can make the choice to stop and get back on the right track. In the following pages

I'll show you how to fill the hollow and keep the old smoking program from coming back. Now we are going to look at your future and point you in a new and exciting direction.

Dealing with the unknown

Fear and doubt can have interesting effects on our behaviour and beliefs. It is a perfectly normal reaction to be wary of change.

A common fear for the smoker considering stopping is 'What will happen to me in the future?'

Fear of the unknown can cause us to resist change. As I mentioned before, knowledge is power. I am helping you by providing all the information you need to effectively stop smoking.

I enjoy teaching people how to juggle as it shows we are all very similar—even the best performers 'drop the ball' every now and then. In learning something new it is inevitable that we will feel confusion, doubt and frustration at some stage. But we persevere. My students see in a short period of time that what they had previously thought was impossible soon comes within reach. Their eyes sparkle as they smile with satisfaction. The brain takes a bit of time to adapt to the new program of juggling the balls but it does adapt. So does the thinking that goes with it.

'Can't' becomes 'Can'.

Do you firmly believe you can stop smoking today?

....

....

People often say to me that they can't juggle. The negative language is the first thing that I encourage them to change before I hand them a ball. They must say with conviction that they can juggle and when I am convinced they are ready, we will short the session. The positive and reinforcing language breaks down the mental barriers and the mind begins to accept the new program that I introduce piece by piece. Very soon the person is juggling three balls just like in the circus. Just like you will stop smoking.

It is likely that there may be days when you are having a tough time of maintaining the change. You may find that your focus is hard to sustain and you know where you should be going but your mind will be trying to force you down the old familiar path of smoking again.

Be aware and make a plan to deal with the bad days. If you feel you are getting frustrated or disappointed then decide now to create a 'break program'.

What can you do to distract your mind when you become frustrated or 'drop the ball'?

Can you stop what you are doing and have a glass of water or take the dog for a walk to have some clear thinking time away from outside influences? Can you stand in front of the mirror and pull some funny faces at yourself (it's a great way to make yourself smile or laugh)?

Making the simple effort to smile will change how you feel and shift your focus.

Create a plan to tackle the challenges and they won't seem so daunting when they do arrive. With a plan of attack in place you'll be able to take them on face to face and you'll come out victorious.

Looking forward

I am a strong believer in looking forward to the road ahead and believe that you can never get enough of a good thing. All successful people talk about goal setting, but what is it?

Goal setting is simply defining what you would like to have happen in your life. It's the process of clarifying your direction.

All of the 'paths to success' books talk about goal setting in some form. You may be thinking 'Oh no, not again!'

The funny thing about goals and goal setting is that even though we all know about them and know what we should be doing, very few people actually follow through and write down what they want to have and achieve.

Tell me, when you drive a car do you just get in and start driving without knowing where you are going? No. Ninety-nine per cent of the time we know where we are going—we either know the way or we get out our road map or GPS. The fact is that there is some sort of plan and there is almost always some sort of goal.

Now you're going to move ahead, you need to know where you are going.

So, if goals are like a road map for your life, where do you want to go with it? What are five things you have been considering that you would like to have happen in your life? Write them down.

....

....

Your goals can be anything from a particular car to living in a certain suburb or town and even personality traits such as gaining self-confidence.

Now, have a look and tell me how you feel about seeing them physically written down. You've taken your desires and goals out of your head and placed them physically on paper.

Does that make your desired direction seem a bit more real and achievable?

Do you feel differently about your goals?

Are you looking at your goals and thinking about other things that you could do in conjunction with them? Write them down now in the space below.

....

....

Making clear goals is just an easy way to get what you want sooner. Writing down what you would like to have happen will clarify your direction.

If you want to cross a river then your goal is to reach the other side. You will need to set your sights on the far bank but also on each individual stepping stone that you will need to step on in order to complete the crossing. Can you see the steps you need to take in order to achieve your goals?

Do you need to get a picture of your favourite car or your dream home so that you have something to focus on?

Would it be a fun and rewarding challenge to enrol in a public speaking course to improve your social skills and your confidence?

What can you do today to start across the river? What is your first step?

....

....

You can now make plans and start taking steps to ensure your goals become a reality.

The power of belief

Picturing yourself at the finish line and brandishing the trophy is very important in the process of training your subconscious mind to actually work with you to achieve your goals. You need to give yourself a clear picture of what you would like to attain.

When I was 14 years old I was introduced to the power of visualisation by my karate sensei. He taught me to integrate my imagination with my conscious mind to create images of karate techniques that I wanted to master. Interestingly enough, within two years I was a sensei myself teaching people the same technique.

You might have made previous attempts to become a non-smoker. These past efforts may be affecting your ability to clearly see your impending success. If you want to become a non-smoker and improve your life, ensure your inner voice is positive and focused on your goals. Your subconscious and conscious mind may be in conflict which can affect the outcome you desire. Let's resolve this conflict right now.

It's common for your conscious mind to say, 'I'm reading this book and I'm aware there are changes that should be made', yet your subconscious responds with something such as, 'It sounds good but remember when you tried last time? You failed then so why would it work now? Are you going to do just the same thing again and waste time?'

You now need to work out why your past attempts didn't work for you.

Did you clearly decide to become a non-smoker when you tried to stop last time?

Were you totally committed to your decision?

....

....

Did you inform the people around you of your decision
and did they support you?

....

....

Did you follow all of the instructions that were given to you
or did you take a few short-cuts to save time or effort?

....

....

Did you believe in yourself and your ability to succeed?

....

....

Take a moment now to remember the last time you
succeeded at something. Did people come up and
congratulate you? Were you patted on the back and did
someone thank you for your great work and perseverance?
Did you receive a reward or did you treat yourself to
something new? Did you feel on top of the world? Did you
feel powerful, as though you could accomplish anything?

....

....

How powerful do you think you will feel after you have beaten smoking forever?

....

....

The way you talk to yourself, your inner dialogue, will play an important part in your success.

What do you tell yourself on a regular basis?

....

....

Do you berate yourself when you make a mistake? Do you say things such as, 'That was a stupid thing to do, gosh I am so stupid'? Or even 'I keep making these mistakes, I am such a loser'? What words and language do you use?

....

....

Do you hold yourself in high regard at all times? Do you treat yourself with love and respect?

....

....

What beliefs could be limiting or stopping you from forging ahead?

....

....

Do you believe you can become a non-smoker today and have no troubles throwing away an old program?

....

....

One of the foundation elements of Western philosophy is the statement 'I think, therefore I am'. One of the most powerful statements you can make in your life will begin with 'I am'. If the sentence begins with 'I am' then the words that follow will create a very deep imprint upon your psyche. If you speak to yourself in a self-defeating manner then the results will be self-defeating behaviour. It's simple. Treating yourself with respect, self-belief and power will allow your mind to create strong pathways towards avenues of success.

You need to stop berating yourself when you make a mistake and start holding yourself in high regard because every word (even if said in jest) makes an imprint upon the sea of unlimited potential that surrounds you. Take away any negative thoughts and forgive yourself for past mistakes. You can delete the useless 'junk' thoughts, the 'what ifs', and by doing so you can clear your mind to make room for the thoughts and processes that are going to empower and strengthen you.

To clear your mind of the old 'junk' you can use the power of forgiveness for yourself and for others. Through forgiveness you'll find that your mind will step forwards and move on instead of holding on and replaying the old thoughts like regret, dislike, hatred or anger. By retaining negative thoughts and energy you can create unwarranted tension and problems in your body and mind. These can be translated as pain, headaches, muscular tension and joint problems. The negative energy can also accumulate and compound in its effects in the internal organs creating problems with the day-to-day operation of the bodily functions. These problems can manifest themselves as indigestion, organ failure or even cancer. This negative energy can be transferred to the people close to you in the way that you communicate with them and with the world around you. They may soon 'feel' the way that you are 'feeling' and so the compounding effects and transference of energy can be visibly measured.

Are there any family members whom you could make amends with? I have a dear friend who recently sought to forgive his family for past misdeeds. He is now enjoying regular outings with them and is able to witness his nephew grow up. I can see in his eyes and his 'spark' a huge weight has been lifted and he is truly enjoying himself and loving his life.

Is there someone you need to forgive?

....

....

Forgiving others is vital but forgiving yourself is an important part of moving forwards and ensuring your personal energy is maximised. A lot of people say they would like to be 20 again but know what they know now. It may seem like a nice thought but the doubt and disbelief in your present abilities and achievements becomes undermined. Looking back on your life is great to be able to see what you have learned and I encourage reflection. Be grateful for what you have achieved and done and where it has led you.

All of your decisions in the past were based on your knowledge, feelings, perceptions and thoughts at the time. These things change as we experience life and gain wisdom. Making mistakes and learning from them is usually an important factor in the gaining of wisdom and life skills. It's important to recognise you did your best at the time and if things did turn out to be wrong then be sure to learn from the situation and use that lesson to help with future decisions or help others to avoid the same mistakes. Failing in the past means you are a step closer to your success and are richer and wiser for the experience. You just need to reflect upon your methods, make some small changes and try again until you achieve the result that you desire.

Can you be grateful for those past experiences and the lessons they have taught you? What are you truly grateful for right now?

....

....

What is great about your life that you haven't realised or acknowledged until now?

....

....

Your past experiences have led you to be reading this book right now. Is it chance, coincidence, fate or, dare I say it … destiny? Whatever you believe in, the fact is we are here today to create a fantastic future for you.

No matter what you've done or tried in the past it is what you do now and in the future that matters.

Fill in the following sections with powerful and positive statements about yourself. Relax your mind and allow the positive attributes to flow. Remember, no-one is going to judge you for what you write here — it is simply an exercise for you to realise your positive attributes and talents. If you believe that you are intelligent, patient and a good listener, then write them down. If you believe that you can manage a Fortune 500 company, then be sure to write it down. Have some fun with it and see how many you can come up with.

I believe I am …

....

....

I believe I can …

....

....

Here's a fun exercise to show you how you can make your subconscious and your imagination work for you.

Get a container or a small rubbish bin and place it on the other side of the room.

Now, get a small, soft ball you can throw into the container, basketball style.

Don't throw it yet. What you need to do to make this experiment effective is to sit and look at the container, take in the surroundings and the colours. Now close your eyes and keep that same picture on the back of your eyelids.

Open your eyes again and repeat the process of opening and closing your eyes for several minutes. You will find that the two pictures become one, whether your eyes are open or not.

The next part of the exercise will involve some work on the part of your imagination.

Close your eyes and picture your hand with the ball in it. See your hand retracting and going through the process of throwing and see your hand actually throwing the ball.

Watch the ball in your imagination as it leaves your fingers and flies through the air to land perfectly in the middle of the container. Hear the sound as the ball hits the base.

Make it as real as possible and perform the imagination exercise several times.

When you have done that for a few minutes I want you to really hold that ball and sit on the chair.

Line yourself up with the container and align yourself with the picture you have created in your mind and throw the ball.

Believe the picture in your mind and allow your body to follow the images—just repeat what you have already seen and experienced in your mind.

When I did this myself I scored 30 out of 30 shots.

Now try throwing the ball with your eyes closed.

Eyes open or closed it shouldn't affect the results as long as your mental picture is clear and you believe in yourself.

I found that I missed the container when I doubted myself or I was distracted by other thoughts or happenings around me.

You'll notice that I have placed no emphasis upon 'how' you should throw the ball and there is no mention of technique. Everyone will have a different method of performing a task but it is the results I want you focus on—the destination, goal or result.

The power of your subconscious is incredible and I hope that this exercise shows you how you can apply visualisation to your life.

You really can do anything if you put your mind to it.

One thing we can truly control in our lives is our thoughts.

In my years of fitness training I have seen that what you eat and how much you consume is very important in successfully managing your body. Like our bodies, our minds are extremely important and need a managed, balanced diet if we are to get ahead.

What are you feeding your brain with on a daily basis? What sort of exercise is it getting?

Is it time to take a break from feeding on a diet of doubt and disbelief?

Make your subconscious mind your greatest ally instead of a foe.

Clear communication

The capability to ask questions and voice our desires using the right language and focus gives us the power of control. Asking out loud and with an expectation of receiving an answer unlocks within us the required resources such as:

- enthusiasm

- determination

- resourcefulness

- lateral thinking

- motivation

- thoughtful reflection. When might this opportunity have presented itself to me in the past?

For the message to be effective it requires a two-way line of communication. When communicating with other people you will notice that there needs to be an open line between you and them. The first is a clear line from you to them that allows the desire or question to be communicated. The second is the return line from them to you so that they can clearly convey the answer in a way that you understand.

Have you ever tried to have a conversation with someone in a noisy environment? Has it been easy for both of you to communicate? Has the message or the answer been mixed up or confused?

How much easier is it to communicate with someone when you're both in a quiet location with no distractions and you're both focused?

The effective line of communication needs:

- clear, concise language containing keywords for what you want to achieve

- to come from within and reflect your true desires

- no outside influences or distractions

- positive focus on the task at hand

- to be backed up by your actions, beliefs and convictions

- a two-way line of communication in which you are clear about your desire or question and also clear about receiving the answer.

Focus is a powerful tool when communicating effectively. Instead of focusing on stopping smoking or 'quitting' smoking I'm going to ask you to focus on what you are going to gain now that you no longer are a slave to the old program. If you focus on *stopping smoking* then half of your focal power will be the word smoking and we don't want that. I want you to concentrate on the positive and not the negative. The language and key words you use will be instrumental in determining the power and strength of your focus. If your focus is broad or ambiguous then it won't have the same effect as if it were concentrated into a single beam like a laser.

Our thoughts, feelings and self-talk are our way of imprinting our desires and awareness onto the sea of unlimited potential that surrounds us. With a clear line of communication for the outgoing message and the incoming answer you can open up a dialogue with your sea of unlimited potential. Just as chemical energy can become kinetic energy the energy of our thoughts can be transformed into the energy of our reality—the energy of our thoughts can become matter.

If every action has an equal and opposite reaction then the intensity with which we focus our beliefs and thoughts on the positive outcome will have a direct effect on the power with which we receive it. Be enthusiastic and excited about what you will gain in respect of time, money and health and you will be in receipt of results that will reflect your excitement. Create and maintain the enthusiasm and this upwards spiral will carry you to new heights each and every day.

You have the ability to create your perfect world. You will stop smoking from today and you will stop the formation of your accident chain in respect to smoking. Adding to your list of desires things such as successful relationships, love, happiness, monetary wealth, even empowering personality traits and beliefs will bring you a brilliant quality of life.

Ask the question out loud and the person beside you just may have the answer. Numerous times I have asked a question in open forums and public places and there has always been someone around who has had an experience from which they can offer an answer or a resource from which I could learn.

So how you do you make it all work? Voicing your desires in the positive is a talent that will improve with practice and is one half of the clear communication equation. The language used promotes a positive focus towards the desired outcome. When you use negative language to express a desire to move away from something, in reality you will be moving towards it. The focal power of desires does not pick up on words such as 'can't', 'won't' or 'don't' and instead focuses on the keywords of the message. If you want to stop smoking but think 'I don't want to smoke anymore', the focus will be on the word 'smoke' rather than on the word 'don't'. Stay positive.

Goal setting works well within a timeframe or with a vision of the final result, but don't set the details of 'where', 'when' and 'how' in concrete; this may limit the mind from seeking or accepting the desired result if it comes at a different time or place. If you think back to past goals you have achieved you will probably notice that things tend to happen at the right time and place for you.

Some good examples of desires could be:

- 'My desire is to reach and maintain my healthy goal weight through exercising on a daily basis at the gym, eating a balanced diet of delicious, fresh food, and having lots of fun and meeting new friends who have the same goals and beliefs.'

- 'I desire to travel to Paris to visit the Louvre and see the sights so that I can absorb some of the wonderful history, culture and beauty that Paris provides.'

With a bit of practice the door will open to the new ability of getting clear with your desires. The process of coaching in this book is about opening the doors to a world of knowledge and ability that will allow you to create new goals, desires and patterns of behaviour that will benefit you for a lifetime. The power of clear, focused language will be a talent you'll improve in as you learn to remove confusion and crossed messages. You can take the finest meal in the world and mix it up in a bucket and no-one will be able to guess what it was. This is the same if you mix up your language when voicing your desires. You'll know what is in your bucket but no-one else can be expected to figure it out.

I have seen people place pictures of what they desire in prominent places so that they can be constantly reminded to maintain their focus and voice their desire while using the right language. There are others who write a list that they then place on the mirror in the bathroom so that they see it clearly every time they brush their teeth.

With all of the millions of things going on in our lives it is easy to forget where we are going or to lose our focus. By placing little reminders in prominent places you'll continue to trigger your brain to maintain its sights on your goal and work with you towards your goals no matter what pops up.

What if?

What if you had never started to smoke?

What if you took another job after you left school?

What if you grew up in a different country, perhaps one that wasn't as fortunate as where you are now?

Life can be dominated and clouded by the 'what if' question if you let it.

It can apply to your past, your present and your future and poses a threat to your ability to be able to move forwards. It is one more thing that you need to leave behind you today.

Asking 'What if' takes your focus away from what you desire and poses doubt and regret in the mind. Self-doubt can be your greatest adversary.

You may have made 'mistakes' in the past and have developed blocks and defensive thoughts in order to protect you from making similar mistakes. A common behaviour is to put oneself down for making silly or stupid mistakes. Everyone makes mistakes and they are a great way to learn but you'll need to be aware of the language you use when communicating with yourself.

Problems and challenges will always face us so it's the manner in which we face these problems that will see us through. Face them with a strong sense of belief in yourself and belief in your abilities and you'll come through with perhaps a few more lessons learned and a lot more power than you would if you just stopped and put up barriers.

Decision making

People I have interviewed in researching this book share one thing. During the process of becoming a non-smoker they have all made a positive decision to quit smoking. Acting on that decision and being committed have been the keys to their continued success. Their level of personal integrity has been proven to be a determining factor.

For some reason it seems as though a lot of people find it easier to pass the responsibility on to others with decision making, whether it be what movie to see at the cinema, to menu choices in a restaurant and even larger ones like where to buy an investment property.

Positive decision making is a skill you should practise daily. Even the choice to let someone else decide is a decision that you make, it's just not an empowering one for you.

As a pilot I was trained to make positive decisions. Professional flight training nowadays concentrates upon the ability of the flight crew to analyse the data and make the best decision based on their available resources.

The airlines plan things such as emergency landing fields, turn around points, fuel required and even split-second decisions such as the Go or No-Go point in the take-off run. This planning and preparation makes the pilot's decision-making process in a stressful emergency situation a whole lot easier.

There have been many times in my flying career where I have had to make split-second decisions with some of them being life or death matters. No matter the level of pressure there is always a process to be followed and that is simply a matter of exploring the possibilities and finding a solution. The information I have presented to you in this book has all been in order for you to be able to make an informed decision on stopping smoking today ... right now.

What is important these days is making an informed decision based on knowledge and your beliefs. If your beliefs aren't getting you to where you want to go then it's perfectly all right to change them.

Establish new and empowering beliefs and reasoning.

My years as a health and fitness trainer have shown me a few things. The first is that all of the good intentions in the world mean absolutely nothing without action. Did you know that gyms all over the world experience a massive influx of new members during the months of January and February? There are lots of people out there who have spent hundreds of dollars on a gym membership and yet have not done more than five workouts before never setting foot in the gym again. The fitness centres love this sort of cash — it is money for nothing.

There's nothing insidious in this comment, it's just the human concept of the New Year resolution coming into play. I don't want you to be a New Year 'resolutionist' anymore.

Who invented that silly notion anyway?

If you really want to do something and make a healthy change, why wait until New Year's Eve to implement it?

If you have a good enough reason to change then why not just change straight away?

The time is here to begin the change you would like to make. There is going to be no New Year resolution, no 'next week', no 'tomorrow' — there is only right now.

What are the reasons you have for making the change to becoming a non-smoker?

....

....

I heard one of the best reasons recently. A friend of mine (who has been smoking since he was 14) asked his young daughter what she would like for her birthday. She apparently gave him the sweetest smile and replied she would like for him to stop smoking. Not bad for a five year old.

You now need to make a decision. You are going to cut off any possibility of going back and you will move forward with strength and power. Now is the time to be definite and certain about what you want to achieve by reading this book. In the goal-setting chapter you will have laid out a plan to follow and you should be able to visualise the results of your decision in your mind. You know where you are going and you can and will make it there.

It is now time for you to make your decision and I am going to be confronting here — there is no hiding and there is no other way.

You have to decide right now that you want and need to stop smoking.

It's really that simple.

If you want to keep smoking and you don't have a single ounce of doubt in your mind then you can quite happily close this book and tell everyone without a doubt that you are a confirmed smoker.

So make your decision. Make it right now and be unwavering in your conviction.

If you think you want to continue smoking but you want to read on to see if I can convince you to stop then you will be wasting your time and the potential of this book at this stage. I cannot make you change. I can only guide you through the process. If you are unsure about your decision it's not a bad thing. It just means that now is not your time. Place this book where you can see it as a regular reminder and pick it up when you believe you are ready to go ahead.

My father is a very intelligent man yet his ability to make a solid decision to stop smoking is really holding him back. He has bought numerous books and brought home leaflets from various organisations but has never followed through with his decision.

There have been times when he has tried to 'give up' but the language in that statement is not the best. All of the literature I have read so far has had negative connotations and some have even been downright rude and insulting to the reader. Giving something up, quitting and cutting back are all negative in my mind.

I believe that no-one likes to be called a 'quitter'.

I am not going to ask you to 'give something up' because giving something up is not pleasant. Ask a mother to 'give up' her children (okay, you funny people, I know you're going to say 'have them') but really, the mother will hold on to those children even tighter and find new ways to protect them.

It's just the same as you trying to 'give up' smoking, or 'quit' smoking.

I would like for you to just change the language that you are going to use in this period of transition.

I don't want you to feel as though you are losing something. It is my aim to get you feeling strongly about the gains you are going to make in your life.

What are you going to gain by going through with your decision?

....

....

By no longer smoking cigarettes, what will be the gains you will make to your health? When you have stopped smoking what will your breath and dental health be like?

....

....

How will you enjoy the free time you will create?

....

....

Do you think you could get that promotion at work, or create more success and better opportunities by being more efficient and productive?

....

....

Will you enjoy feeling vibrant and energetic when your clean and healthy lungs feed lots of oxygen into your system?

Will you have fun running and playing with the kids without being out of breath?

Could you wear the same shirt two days in a row if it doesn't smell like smoke? (I won't tell).

Will you enjoy the smell of the salt water at the beach?

Could you enjoy the taste of a nice meal?

When was the last time you *really* tasted a delicious meal?

It has always made me laugh the lengths that smokers go in masking the fact that they have just had a cigarette. In my smoking days I believed that drinking cordial straight from the container would be strong enough to mask the smell.

There is even an entire industry of breath freshener sprays and mints that thrive on the back of this 'smoker guilt'.

The fact is that the smoke gets inhaled into the lungs and apart from jamming an air freshener directly into your lungs there is no way to get rid of the smell, only mask it.

Okay, so here we are.

I would like for you to copy the following sentence in the space provided. Write it for yourself and believe it.

I now do not smoke. I have made an informed decision and believe my decision is the right one for me. I believe in my ability to follow through with strength and conviction and my high level of integrity will allow me to remain steadfast on my new path of healthier behaviour and self-awareness. I will feel and look younger. I will achieve new levels of success in everything I do and I will love my life.

....

....

....

....

....

....

....

....

Chapter 7

YOUR NEW PROGRAM

To know even one life has breathed easier because you have lived; this is to have succeeded.

Ralph Waldo Emerson (1803–1882)

To create a balanced equation in your life you need to not only eliminate the old program but create a new and empowering set of beliefs and behaviours. Your transition will be accepted by both your conscious and subconscious minds and you will have full control over your fresh and enlightened path. This chapter will help you with the tools for your new direction.

The sun rises

When you wake up tomorrow the levels of nicotine in your body will be significantly diminished. Your brain will be sending out a message to ask you to light up a cigarette and your subconscious pattern of behaviour may want to kick in by itself. It will be the best time to consciously reinforce your new empowering program and practise some deep-breathing exercises (I'll show you an effective method at the end of the book).

Be aware of the triggers and the times when you automatically stopped to have a cigarette, take this new found awareness and use it as a tool to create change.

Decide to exchange that first cigarette for a glass of cold, fresh water and some deep breathing. Overnight your body will have dehydrated and will have used its store of energy for the repair phase. With the extra time you have on hand use it to prepare a breakfast that will get you through the morning

You'll have gained some time back by stopping smoking so exchange it for preparing for a great day ahead — make a list of what you need to do or what you would like to achieve.

Use this time to admire the morning outside and listen to the noises of the neighbourhood waking up. Kick a ball and run around with the kids or the dog for 10 minutes.

Head out to the car and clean out the ashtray for the last time.

Make your lunch for the day.

By preparing and planning for your day ahead you'll find that you will create even more time and energy for what you enjoy doing. Your preparation will give you an idea of the challenges you may face which can allow you to be mentally and physically ready to deal with them, get them out of the way easily and reduce your stress.

Learn how to say 'no'

Making a stand and saying 'no' is something you now need to enforce. Saying 'no' does not have to be seen as a selfish act.

Saying 'no' with tact and proper consideration takes a bit of practice so we are going to start here with some exercises. This might seem weird, but what's new?

I'm sure you have heard the term, 'It's not just what you say but how you say it'. It really works and now you're going to try it out.

You'll need to stand for this one and don't worry about what the people in the next room might think, just go for it. This is a great game of pretend where you can give an Oscar winning performance.

Stand up tall and breathe in deeply.

Shake your arms and then shake each leg individually. This is to loosen up the muscles and get the blood flowing.

Now try talking from different parts in your mouth and throat, make your throat go from deep to high and play with the pitch.

Play with this over the next few minutes. Say the following sentence over and again but place the emphasis on each word in turn.

'No, thank you, I don't smoke!'

'*No*, thank you, I don't smoke!'

'No, *thank* you, I don't smoke!'

'No, thank *you*, I don't smoke!'

'No, thank you, *I* don't smoke!'

'No, thank you, I *don't* smoke!'

'No, thank you, I don't *smoke*!'

Put some effort into this and you will notice how differently you feel when you say each emphasised word.

Now say the sentence with a smile on your face.

Try saying it while laughing—even your best fake laugh will do.

How do you feel when you say '*No*'?

Do you feel just a bit more in control?

When you emphasise '*thank*' do you feel differently?

Can you hear the difference in your voice when you emphasise each word in turn?

Do you feel empowered and in control?

We remember

When I was about nine years old I was taught how to juggle. Eventually the juggling balls were put away in a cupboard and after moving house they were lost. I had forgotten all about juggling until one day when I was 26 I came across a store selling juggling equipment. Within minutes I had bought a new set of juggling balls and the proprietor had revived my old skill and taught me a new trick. After so many years the old pattern was able to return almost instantly.

Your body will never forget the act of smoking so if you never want to start again then you need to remove all forms of temptation from your home and work. You need to keep looking forwards and forget this past pattern of behaviour.

Do you remember how you felt before you smoked?

Do you remember a time when you had more energy?

Like our brains our bodies remember what has happened to them in the past. If you were once fit but have let it slip then your body will remember the fit days when you begin training again. Your body will also remember the bad things as well so this is where self-awareness becomes important.

The intake of nicotine is remembered by the receptors in your brain and one puff on a cigarette will switch on the receptors and will reactivate the program of smoking. Even just the act of picking up a lighter or a packet of cigarettes may be enough to activate your memory and allow your old program to wake up. One seemingly innocent cigarette will become two and then the program will start anew. If you have made the decision to become a non-smoker then you must be aware that stepping back and reactivating the physical motions of smoking for even just one puff will see you needing to go through *Escape from Smoking* again.

The accident chain in respect to smoking is added to every day whether you want it to or not. Subconsciously your mind is taking in the messages that surround you and keeps placing links into your chain and weakening existing ones. You can stop this chain formation by removing all forms of temptation. Here are some examples:

- No more hanging out with the smokers at the front of the office building unless you are sure you can resist the urge to have 'just one'. Having a fresh air break can be beneficial in clearing your thoughts but be aware of and resist the temptation of an old program.

- Staying for the entire meal and conversation when entertaining friends and family at a restaurant or at home.

- Not purchasing any cigarettes or other form of tobacco even if it's a favour for your friend or partner.

- Throwing away all of the smoking paraphernalia in and around your home and work. It doesn't matter how much money you have spent on it.

- Ignoring the placement of cigarettes in stores which encourage impulse buys.

- Avoiding or managing stressful situations that may cause a temporary lapse in your resolve.

Just remember to breathe.

Engage with the natural world

The cells in our bodies are continuously dying off and regenerating. Where do we get the replacements? The sea of unlimited potential (Quantum SOUP) theories propose that we are constantly sharing cells with each other and our environment. How we interpret our energy is akin to a television antenna receiving a signal and translating it onto the screen as pictures and sound.

With the prolific electronic energy in the atmosphere I feel that our brains and bodies are becoming distracted. It is becoming easier to lose focus on the simple things, the good stuff in life. A great example can be seen in large shopping centres and malls. The bright displays, lighting, music and background noise are all part of a plan to distract your focus and cause you to spend more money than you might have planned. Take some time to consider your environment and surroundings. Most importantly take the time to slow down and listen to your body and the way it is interpreting the signals both internally and externally.

Through personal experience I have observed that, rather than exchanging energy with the artificial manufactured environments we live in and are exposed to every day, it is beneficial to exchange energy and draw strength from powerful, natural beings such as:

- trees and forests

- oceans and beaches

- deserts

- lakes and rivers

- rock formations.

Where do you spend your days?

....

....

How do you spend your free time?

....

....

The lost art of breathing

Watch martial artists go through their patterns and moves and you will see that the physical movement is paired with a correct and practised breathing pattern, something that has been developed over many years. Disciplines such as yoga, tai chi and Pilates make the breath their main focus.

The interesting thing about the use of cigarettes when feeling under pressure is that the user takes a deep breath when inhaling the smoke. Is it the cigarette that produces the relaxing affect or the deep breath?

Unfortunately a link is made that connects the cigarette to the feeling of relief. The influx of nicotine into the system and starving the brain of oxygen also fools the brain into a sense of peace and comfort.

Take the time now to take a deep breath and see how it feels. Sit tall and breathe in deeply, filling your lungs with fresh air.

No, really, try it.

Sit tall, perhaps even stand up so that your diaphragm can expand fully.

How do you feel after one breath?

....

....

Did you feel that your eyes brightened, your hearing improved and you suddenly became aware of your surroundings?

Now take a deep breath and hold it in for about five to 10 seconds. Breathe out and really empty your lungs. Push every bit of air out. Keep pushing the air out until there is absolutely no more and your body heaves a huge breath in. How do you feel now?

....

....

Think back to five minutes ago, how was your breathing? Was it deep and controlled or shallow?

....

....

Take the time to repeat the deep breathing 10 times.

How do you think you will feel if you do that regularly?

....

....

The amount of oxygen you take in doing this sort of breathing is phenomenal. Your blood will become oxygen rich and you will benefit from it right down to the very last cell.

Next time you are feeling stressed or uptight stop and take note of how you are breathing.

Take the time to stop and perform five deep breaths and see how that affects your stress level and your ability to think clearly.

Deep breathing is a great way to relax your body to reduce stress or make it ready for sleep.

Celebrate the wins

So, what do you do now? Let's have a little celebration.

Grab your packet of cigarettes and tell them that you no longer want or need them.

I want to hear you say it! Say it with conviction. Come on! This isn't just a silly trick. No-one is watching. Say you don't want or need them with some real authority. Use a commanding tone because now you are in command, you're in control of your own thoughts and actions.

Now, take the cigarettes out of the packet and tear the filters off one by one and toss each cigarette into the bin.

You've spent a lot of money on these cigarettes and may want to give them to someone who does still smoke — resist that urge. You've spent a fortune over the years so these last few dollars will become symbolic in your quest for freedom. Don't give them away easily, you must destroy them.

Tell each cigarette that you no longer want it and you no longer need it. Don't just think it, verbalise it. Hear yourself say it out loud.

Doesn't that feel great?

Do you feel relieved?

Now, put a huge smile on your face and exclaim:

'I am free, I have stopped smoking forever. I am free. I am in control.'

Hear it, feel it and believe it!

The end and the beginning

Now that you have nearly finished reading this book from cover to cover it is time to create your main reference page.

Your eyes are now open to a new world of possibilities so keep them open and be receptive to new ideas, opportunities and answers. This is akin to an awakening. You are now well on the way to living a positively balanced life so perhaps you can help or teach another.

What is your motivation for stopping smoking?

....

....

How confident are you of your ability to stop right now? (Circle a number)

0   1   2   3   4   5   6   7   8   9   10

Not confident   Highly confident

How confident are you in your ability to make decisions and follow through with the actions required?

0   1   2   3   4   5   6   7   8   9   10

Not confident   Highly confident

Have you followed all of the instructions and completed all of the exercises in this book?

Yes   No

Do you know what to do if you feel as though you are slipping or feeling lost?

Yes   No

Who is your support for your transition?

....

....

How much are you going to put into your efforts to consciously remain a non-smoker?

(Circle a number)

0   1   2   3   4   5   6   7   8   9   10

No effort   Everything I've got

Do you feel in control of your body and your mind?

             Yes   No

After you have answered all of the questions on these two pages you'll need to do the following:

• Keep the book open at these pages and turn it over.

• Place it beside your bed.

• Make sure you refer to it as soon as you wake up tomorrow morning and each morning thereafter.

As a reminder for your journey I have used the four ancient elements to create a simple mantra.

Earth — You are now more in tune with yourself and the world around you — use your connection wisely.

Air — Remember to breathe.

Fire—Use it only for preparing food and heating.

Water—Drink plenty.

Congratulations on making it this far and for completing the program.

Index

If you really enjoyed this book, please help us to help others by recommending it to a friend or family member.

Let us know your story.

Internet: <www.escapefromsmoking.com>

Email: info@mpoweruaustralia.com.au

Subject: Escape from Smoking